www.kamerabooks.co.uk

Colin Odell & Michelle Le Blanc

HORROR FILMS

Kamera
BOOKS

First published in 2007 by Kamera Books
PO Box 394, Harpenden, Herts, AL5 1XJ
www.kamerabooks.com

Copyright © Colin Odell & Michelle Le Blanc, 2007
Series Editor: Hannah Patterson

Index and proofing: Richard Howard

A CIP catalogue record for this book is available from the British Library.

ISBN-10: 1-84243-218-4
ISBN-13: 978-1-84243-218-1

Typeset by Avocet Typeset, Chilton, Aylesbury, Bucks
Printed by SNP Lefung Printers (Shenzen) Co Ltd, China

For Alice, our furry feline friend, who watched thousands of films over the thirteen years she lived with us. She snoozed through all the films you're about to read about, but sadly passed away five days before the deadline for this book. We miss her very much.

ACKNOWLEDGEMENTS

Our thanks to the usual suspects for welcome distractions and many other things – Paul, Lizbeth and And, and Gavin and Hanako. A big hello to Graham and Kirsty, and a special mention for Graham's car keys and the endoscope. Thanks to Claire and Mark for their international bookspotting activities. For all their support our thanks and love to Tony, Christine and Marc Le Blanc and Truus Odell. Also thanks to Hannah Patterson, Ion Mills, Antonio Pasolini and Xavier Mendik.

CONTENTS

INTRODUCTION

Catch catch the horror taxi
I fell in love with a video nasty
Catch catch the horror train
Freeze frame gonna drive you insane

The axe is sharp and the blade is keen
Creature features, spirits on your screen
Shadows fall, in all this gloom
You're not so safe
In the safety of your room

                              Nasty – The Damned

The horror film has a fearsome reputation, dismissed by critics and pillo-ried by the media. Yet it is hugely popular, diverse in content and as old as cinema itself. In this book we will provide an overview of this most detested of genres, covering its history and examining the key figures who have shaped the horror film into the multi-faceted beast it has become. There is a whole world of scary cinema out there, but no way that a book of this size can be exhaustive, especially given the moun-tains of often-variable product in even the most modest DVD rental store. So we take a selective look at films and movements that will offer a feel and understanding of the genre and explain why – rather than simply stoke the fires of media outrage – it can serve a higher purpose.

Despite scare stories that horror is a new scourge demonising the young, it has, in fact, a rich literary and oral heritage that stretches far into the past. It is one of the most enduring forms of storytelling precisely because it deals in primal fears – and learning to fear is essential to any animal that has successors in the food chain. The oldest surviving extant poem in the English language, *Beowulf* (c. Eighth century), is at heart a gruesome horror tale. Horror had progressed into an artform that stepped away from the simple morality of traditional tales. The addition of the supernatural or extra-natural to the mix provided a narrative hook as well as a spiritual element that linked religion and morality. Many horror stories explore the nature of faith or have overt religious connotations – their purpose is to justify prescribed behaviours as much as show the effects of transgressions from them.

Horror also has a secondary purpose: to confront primordial fears in a safe environment, preparing an individual for a cruel world and providing a cautionary source of morality in an entertaining manner. Horror tales, be they oral or cinematic, are told in the dark or at night where the logical light of day cannot disperse their phantasmagorical effect or mock their inherently dubious premises. It is no accident that horror films are inherently scarier in a darkened cinema than in an ordinary living room. The horror film offers the audience an experience of fear and disgust within a non-threatening context; whatever fear is irrationally felt, they rationally acknowledge that the film itself cannot physically cause them harm, short of being decapitated by a flying reel of IMAX stock. There is a catharsis within horror – the audience can see victims deal with a situation, jump at the scary moments and recoil at the grotesque, but ultimately leave the cinema unscathed. This also makes the horror film ideal for dating, and a particularly popular genre among teenagers. Horror also offers a form of relief at times of stress, either personal or on a wider societal scale. Like comedy, a genre that it is closely related to, horror portrays a situation that is worse than any you might currently face. And there is comfort in knowing that, however bad your lot may be, for the 90 minutes you are in the cinema you can watch someone else having a far worse time.

Although the roots of the horror story can be seen in literary and oratory traditions, film is, by its nature, a visual medium and further precedents come from the world of art and theatre. Early cave paintings, the imaginatively gruesome atrocities portrayed by Bruegel and Bosch, the fear of the natural world in the Sublime canvases of the late eighteenth century or the distorted realities of Hogarth all have a part to play in the evolution of visualising the grotesque or frightening. More recently, the advent of psychoanalysis pre-empted the rise of the Surrealist movement with its dreamlike, occasionally nightmarish imagery. The sexual alien sadism of HR Giger or the grotesques of Francis Bacon also provide starting points for visual expression in the moving arts. And yet cinema still struggles to be accepted as an artform in its own right and the horror film has the hardest task of all, despite the miasma of sub-genres and styles that make it an incredibly rich part of world cinematic heritage. Horror, for the most part, remains the province of the aficionado rather than the critic, with positive criticism generally justified by rebranding the product – you are unlikely to find works by Bergman, Pasolini or Buñuel in the horror section of your local DVD store despite the fact they have all made horror films. But its continued popularity suggests that people will part with their money time and again for the privilege of being scared witless.

So, what is it that makes a horror film? As with all genres the label is a loose generalisation designed to characterise visual or thematic elements that typify a product in the mind of the consumer. These include the structure, the monster, the thrill and the relationship of the film to the viewer.

'WE HAVE SUCH SIGHTS TO SHOW YOU'[1] THE HORROR FILM'S STRUCTURE

Thomas Schatz, in his seminal work on Hollywood genres, states that 'genre experience, like all human experience, is organised according to certain fundamental perceptual processes. As we repeatedly undergo the same type of experience we develop expectations which, as they are continually reinforced, tend to harden into "rules".'[2] The purpose of a genre is to provide a clear structure that the audience will recognise, and while Schatz does not demean himself to discuss the horror film in his book, the genre's main aim is to elicit fear within the viewer.

The basic structure of the horror film is a three-step construction of order, chaos and reconstruction, with an optional bookending device or prologue. The purpose is to show a society or microcosm thereof dealing with catastrophic change, usually inflicted by a monster, the perpetrator that elicits a marked emotional response from the viewer. The monster need not be an actual physical beast, rather it is the catalyst for the chaos inflicted. The structure of the horror film determines how the society goes about reconstructing a semblance of order. The opening act depicts an internally ordered society (not necessarily a good order but with boundaries of accepted normality) unaware of impending disruption. This can be a 'normal town' (*The Virgin Spring*, *Halloween*, *Gremlins*), an isolated group (*Evil Dead Trap*, *Alien*, *The Thing*, *Deliverance*, *Friday the 13th*) or an individual (*Carrie*, *The Vanishing*). This establishes the environment and shows stability. This stability is disrupted by the addition of the monster, the chaotic element that breaks down the demarcation of social order. It is the core of the film and defines it as horror. Finally there is the reconstruction or resolution where society returns to a stable form. Crucially, this stability may not be the same as that which established the film, and it isn't necessarily good. Success for the monster can create a new order that is internally stable but hardly desirable – it is the alteration and the process of reconstruction that provides the genre's basic narrative drive. The only addition to this basic structure is either a bookending device (*The Fog*, *The Cabinet of Dr Caligari*), a shock ending that occurs apparently after the restoration of order (*Carrie*) or a prologue (*Halloween*). The latter is often used as a portent of things to come (like a mini trailer), a justification of the monster or as a way of keeping the audience tense, aware that they are watching a horror film and not a drama. Most films follow this three-section structure although some try to counter it by employing downbeat endings (*Night of the Living Dead*, *The Birds*) that offer no solution to the problem, effectively ending in chaos. But this chaos is now established and has become the template for the society portrayed. *Dawn of the Dead* appears to be set entirely in the middle, chaotic segment but internally follows the three-section structure. Similarly some films (notably *Saw III* and the notorious *Guinea Pig* series) apparently dispense with establishing an order to disorientate their audience, providing a reactionary environment for atrocity over narrative cohesion; but even these provide a resolution by their conclusions.

'IT'S ALIVE! IT'S ALIVE!'[3] SUB-GENRES AND HORROR THEMES

The horror film is particularly malleable and can accommodate other genre types, often merging with science fiction, thriller or fantasy, making it difficult to categorise. Occasionally films that are clearly horror are placed under different categories so as not to be tarnished by the label. *Alien* is branded as science fiction and not a haunted house film in space, while *Se7en* is apparently a thriller rather than a reworking of *The Abominable Dr Phibes*. Similarly, there are films that are undeniably horrific but are not usually described as horror in the generic sense of the term – Steven Spielberg's PG-rated films *Jaws* and *Jurassic Park* are horror films, but the more visceral *Munich* and *Saving Private Ryan* are not. What sets these apart is the presence of a defined monster. There are many kinds of monsters and sub-genres but they generally fall into one or more of four categories, although each of these is subject to cross-fertilisation and amalgamation.

Natural: Nature represents a primal fear. It is chaotic, unpredictable and often as violent as it is beautiful. Man's insignificance in the universe is epitomised by futile attempts at controlling its forces. The greatest fear lies with that which we cannot understand and nature is the first manifestation of this. The ecological horror film shows the effects of the planet on humankind, either as punishment for meddling (*The Host*, *Them!*), the primitive attacking the modern which upsets the balance of evolution (*Jaws*, *Grizzly*) or man as insignificant to the greater purpose of nature's slow cycle (*Volcano*, *Armageddon*). This sub-genre sometimes crosses with the scientific monster – for example, the electrically awoken worms of *Squirm* or the genetics tampering of *Piranha* or *Jurassic Park*. Resolution is often achieved by scientific means (*The Swarm*), confrontation which re-establishes the protagonist's link with his/her primitive self (*Jaws*, *Moby Dick*) or by nature simply running its course (*Earthquake*).

Supernatural: It is far easier to dismiss supernatural horror as fantastical because cold logic requires empirical evidence of its existence, but paradoxically this can also be its power. The supernatural monster is either a fantastical bogeyman that cannot rationally exist and can therefore be dismissed or it can represent religious spirituality that can affect a person's soul and therefore be more metaphysically resonant. Vampires, werewolves and zombies allow the audience to have their cake and eat it – they can enjoy the scares then dismiss the monsters at their leisure. Many supernatural creatures are based on religious mythologies or folklore. Associated with these are prescribed means of dispatch, although the cinematic form will often expand, develop or defy them. Less easy to dismiss are demonic possession films, as these are concerned with the violation of the body and the soul – there is more at stake in *The Exorcist* than corporeal violation. Supernatural monsters, because of their unfathomable and enigmatic nature, also allow the filmmaker to let their imagination run riot, creating terrors outside our waking reality. Clive Barker's Cenobites from *Hellraiser* or the demons of *Jigoku* come from twisted, distorted worlds far beyond our comprehension.

Psychological: Perhaps one of the more terrifying monsters, the psychotic killer is usually based entirely in the real world. Sub-genres from the thriller to the slasher have relied on the evil or madness of a vicious perpetrator to elicit their thrills. Sometimes they are given an excuse or a reason for their actions – whether it be abuse at the hands of the father (*Peeping Tom*), a frightening Oedipal complex (*Maniac, Psycho*) or being simply driven to madness by noisy neighbours (*Driller Killer*). In these cases the audience may not be able to identify with the monster, but can at least understand it. Occasionally there is no obvious cause or explanation for a killer's crimes (*Henry, Portrait of a Serial Killer*) or sometimes it's the chilling motivation of someone wanting simply to know how it feels to kill (*The Sailor Who Fell from Grace with the Sea, Spoorloos*). Stories can be taken from the news, or just claim to be based on true events to provide extra chills – *The Texas Chain Saw Massacre* was (very) loosely based on the Ed Gein killings, *Wolf Creek*, apparently, on a number of prominent murder cases. Killers are difficult to dismiss when today's sensationalist press turns real life crimes into hard-hitting narratives that ultimately exploit the victims; but their effect on the public psyche is hard to ignore. It is only when crossed with the supernatural that they become easier to deal with (Michael Myers in *Halloween*).

Scientific: A popular staple of the genre is the mad scientist, with a brilliant mind yet fanatically driven, blinkered vision that can lead to all sorts of evil, whether it be accidental or intentional. Dr Jekyll, Dr X, Fu Manchu and Professor Quatermass have all created terrifying progeny of science. Frankenstein's monster is a product of a man's obsessive determination to create life from dead flesh, but who is really the monster – the creation or the creator? Concerns about the threat of the atom bomb and the destruction of the world through the clinical and relentless pursuit of science reflected very real fears of the time; both the ants of *Them!* and *Gojira* are brought into being by the atomic bomb. What's interesting about the latter is that, while it is ultimately science that saves the day, it also explores the ethical considerations of using science for evil as well as good. Speculative or science fiction-based horror also offers cautionary tales of well-meaning research gone wrong, a trait particularly common in the films of David Cronenberg, but it would be wrong to think of these films as somehow Luddite – in many ways they uphold the ethos of progress through daring invention, even if the initial test results go awry.

'THE WORLD IS SO DIFFERENT IN THE DAYLIGHT. BUT AT NIGHT, YOUR FANTASIES GET OUT OF HAND.'[4] – THE MECHANICS OF THE SCARES

As with all movies horror films have a specific language that the audience subconsciously learns how to read. The film *Scream*, for example, knowingly explains the plot mechanics of the slasher movie whilst itself being a film of that sub-genre. These conventions are all part of the mechanism of developing the scare. Although they can be broken or twisted, it must be within the rules of narrative cinema, so that the audience remains aware of the plot's direction. Even if they are wrong-footed, temporarily or permanently, it is generally within the parameters of standard narrative convention, to emphasise the meaning of the film. Horror's main aim is to elicit fear, terror or an unnerving sense of unease in the viewer, and there are many techniques that the director, and the sound and film editors, can employ when it comes to generating tension and pacing.

One of the simplest ways to create fear is by not showing anything at all. The shot of a single face screaming in terror, for example, can trigger the viewer to imagine a cause more horrifying than any director could show. This method can also be used to get a lower certification or simply to disguise a modest effects budget. When employed cleverly (*Curse of the Cat People*, *The Haunting*), the effect is truly spine chilling. However, such means do not always sustain a sense of fear for the entire running time and often the filmmaker is forced to show some form of monster, lest the audience feel cheated.

There are fundamental differences between tension, suspense and shock. Hitchcock was renowned for using suspense in films that, bar a couple, would not conventionally be considered horror pictures, but the effect of the technique remains the same. In the classic text *Hitchcock by Truffaut*, Hitchcock explains the difference between surprise and suspense by reference to a hypothetical film scenario involving a bomb under a table in a restaurant. In one film the audience is unaware of the bomb, in the other they are not: 'In the first case we have given the public fifteen seconds of surprise at the moment of the explosion. In the second we have provided them with fifteen minutes of suspense. The conclusion is that wherever possible the public must be informed.'[5]

Hitchcock's perceptions on the difference between surprise and suspense are acute but sometimes the surprise is what the audience want, the thrill of the quick adrenaline rush caused by a sudden, unexpected shock. The technique of using tension plays somewhere between suspense and shock and is extremely important in the horror genre, the filmic equivalent of misdirection in a particularly good magic trick. Tension is created by giving the audience a hint of what could happen, but not letting on when or how. Tension can be used on both a filmic level and a scenic level. Horror films tend to play tension one of two ways on a filmic level. The first is to slowly build the horror, dropping clues and subtle hints, with each confrontation becoming nastier right up to the final showdown (*The Omen* effect). The other device is completely opposite and shows all the nastiness right at the start, confronting the audience head on. There is no need to show further terror to the same degree, because the tension is established. The audience know how nasty things can get, but are still completely in the dark as to how much worse it could be (the *Maniac* effect). On a scenic level tension provides an intense feeling in the audience – that 'edge of the seat' feeling. They are fully aware that something bad is going to happen but are forced to wait. Think of the diving scene in *Jaws*, the kitchen sink sequence in *A Tale of Two Sisters* or any scene where a lone, jittery person (usually a woman) walks down a dank corridor. Music, or lack of it, often plays a vital role in creating this kind of tension.

The technique of shock is occasionally preceded by tension but doesn't have to be – take the bus death scene in *Final Destination*, for example. Red herrings are, naturally, obligatory in most productions – why go for a complicated scare when a false alarm is just as effective? This is known as 'the bus', a term which derives from Jacques Tourneur's *Curse of the Cat People*. After an interminably tense walk through a park where we are convinced the protagonist is going to be savagely attacked, the hiss of a bus's brakes causes the audience to leap out of their seats. The scene concludes with safety for the character and a massive shock for the audience, who expected a far less fortunate outcome. Similar uses are made of cats (*Alien*) or, popular in modern horrors, two people bumping into each other in a school corridor, always accompanied by an accentuating musical 'dah-dah!' that provides a cheap shock without any actual consequence.

Essential to the maintaining of suspense, tension or shock is the use of music and sound effects, or occasionally lack thereof. The aforementioned shot of a jittery figure walking down a corridor can be enhanced immeasurably by either the simple echoes of her footsteps and the drip-drip of a broken pipe, or by an ominous score. Similarly, shock can be generated by a deliberately loud foley effect or a sudden atonal orchestral crash. Tension can be elicited by a steady increase in the music's rhythm and tempo, which causes the audience to imagine that a grisly conclusion to the scene is imminent. Foley effects enhance any scenes of bloodshed or mayhem, the simple sound of a cabbage being sliced can give the impression of someone being decapitated – it is the marriage of sound and visuals that create the overall effect. Often foley effects can be used to imply violent action that occurs offscreen or make apparently innocuous activities appear grotesque, for example, the dumpling eating scenes from Fruit Chan's *Dumplings*.

'MOVIES DON'T CREATE PSYCHOS, THEY JUST MAKE THEM MORE CREATIVE'[6] – THE VIEWER'S RELATIONSHIP TO THE HORROR FILM

The complex relationship between viewer and screen provides a variety of conflicts that form the tone and emphasis of a particular film. This isn't exclusive to horror, but the way in which various viewpoints are mixed dictates the overall feel of a piece and marks the film as horrific. Key to the success lies with the director's ability to appeal to an audience's emotional response rather than a logical one – the medium is inherently artificial so the viewer's suspension of disbelief is vital if the film is to have resonance. The three primary modes of audience relationship to the screen in the horror film are: voyeur, victim and violator.

Voyeur: The privileged spectator watches the acts of terror from a detached viewpoint. The enjoyment lies in the spectacle or the relaying of the story. The advantaged viewpoint allows us to see events that are denied the protagonists, for example, the viewer is made aware of a killer waiting patiently in a darkened room while the victim is unaware of his presence. Linked with voyeurism is scopophilic desire and, conversely, helplessness that derives from being outside narrative intervention. However, the detached viewpoint can result in a disinterested perspective, which allows the audience the luxury of viewing the film at an aesthetic level, removing any personal attachment to the characters. Although this position is generally undesirable in a horror film, as character empathy makes the experience more thrilling, there are exceptions: in Jörg Buttgereit's *Der Todesking*, aesthetic distancing pushes matters into the arena of the art film and renders the morbid events less exploitational.

Victim: Empathy with the character and experiencing the action from their viewpoint occasionally makes the viewer the surrogate victim of the horror. While the advantaged viewpoint leaves the spectator helpless, there is at least no direct threat to them, but from the victim's point of view this is not the case. In *The Texas Chain Saw Massacre* when

Sally regains consciousness we watch (as she does) the ogling faces of the cannibal family who have captured her. In a sense we have become her for that moment.

Violator: The camera as killer is a popular component of the horror film from *Peeping Tom* to *Halloween* and *Wolfen*. The viewer sees as the killer does and becomes implicated in the perpetration of the atrocity. This aspect has created much of the outrage against stalk 'n' slash films of the early 1980s, when it was argued that viewing through the killers' eyes reinforced the misogynist attitudes of these pictures and somehow encouraged the spectator to align with this way of thinking. Associating with the killer through their point of view can create paradoxical reactions and meanings for the viewer – on one hand we become the killer and are granted the privileged position of seeing the murder, but simultaneously we are distanced from the act because these actions are pre-determined by the film's director. This technique can be used not only to identify with the killer but also to hide their identity, a common device in giallo films where the subjective viewpoint provides empathetic thrills but denies the revelation of the murderer.

These three devices do not necessarily remain isolated. In *Henry: Portrait of a Serial Killer*, Henry and Otis abuse and butcher a family. We see the scene, without cuts, from the point of view of a camcorder that is recording the slaughter, initially as violator (the scene begins with the camera handheld) before becoming a detached voyeur (as the camera is abandoned so its operator can join in the murder). Sometimes all three techniques are used simultaneously. In the prom massacre sequence in *Carrie* the scene is played in split-screen so we simultaneously view the carnage from afar, from Carrie's viewpoint and from her victims' perspective. Knowingly cinematic, the result makes the viewer at once voyeur, victim and violator.

'CENSORS TEND TO DO WHAT ONLY PSYCHOTICS DO: THEY CONFUSE REALITY WITH ILLUSION.'[7] – CENSORSHIP AND THE SCARY MOVIE

Almost all countries have some form of classification or censorship system, even if it is voluntary. The history of the horror film is tied up with that of censorship in a number of ways. Horror is considered to be lowbrow entertainment even in cinematic terms and calls have always existed for the establishment to curtail excesses in popular arts or impose some kind of morality code. Censorship creates problems for the horror filmmaker as different taboos are given different weight in different countries – what is acceptable in one country can be banned in another. But whatever these difficulties, horror's relationship with the censors has driven the market in various directions. A film like *King Kong* would not have had the same level of violence had it been made a few years later when the Hays Code (a code of morality designed to curtail the decadent excesses of Tinseltown at a time of authoritarian Puritanism) had fully been implemented in 1934. It is interesting to note also the difference in tone between *Frankenstein* and its sequel *Bride of Frankenstein*, which were respectively made either side of this implementation. This code of morality effectively restricted depictions of sex and violence on American cinema screens. In the UK the BBFC (British Board of Film Censorship, now Classification) had its own, occasionally bizarre, approach to censorship that has been at times far more arbitrary than its American counterpart the (superficially voluntary) MPAA, even taking artistic merit into account as a criterion for classifying films.

The collapse of the American studio system in the late 1960s heralded a new era of unbridled sex and violence in the States. On the surface the relaxation of censorship seemed just to offer a carnival of excess, but there were also political and radical considerations. The breakdown (albeit temporarily) of censorship guidelines regarding feature films in the USA certainly allowed for a greater degree of exploitation, viscera and even, briefly, the mainstream acceptance of hardcore pornography, but, more importantly, it also allowed people to criticise the political process. The emergence of the counterculture movement and the increasingly bloody and desperate state of affairs in Vietnam provided the impetus for a slew of horror films that used this new found freedom to criticise the government in a way that would reach people not normally exposed to political allegory. In Spain the horror film (and even films about horror films, such as *Spirit of the Beehive*) was the only way that political allegory could be distilled to the masses under the oppressive Franco regime – its fantastic nature allowing it to sink beneath the radar of the authorities. It is a trend that was adopted in many countries, especially those that viewed the films as beyond contempt and hence beyond concern. While many horror films are just made for exploitation or simply entertainment purposes the links between political subversion and the horror film are strong, providing an alternative to reactionary state entertainment and showing a mirror to society's concerns. It's a strange situation that has some markets censoring horror films for their visual content, while in some countries filmmakers use the genre to bypass censorship of politically subversive commentary.

Whatever the reason for censorship it has created a market amongst aficionados for films to be seen in their original state (i.e. uncut), a situation particularly notable in the UK following the notorious 'video nasties' panic in the early 1980s. The start of the home video boom had caught the authorities by surprise. There was no regulated form of censorship for video and a moral panic was unleashed by the tabloid newspapers outraged by the availability of such notorious titles as *Cannibal Ferox* and *The Beast in Heat*. Following a series of trials the decision was made to censor videos in the same manner as film, but on a far stricter basis – due to their availablity in any living room and the viewer's ability to pause the 'good bits' – resulting in nearly two decades of mangled content. This situation has, to a large extent, now changed, although the legacy of these early witch-hunts can still be felt. The worldwide nature of the Internet has made it easier to obtain full prints of films for home viewing, although there are still restrictions that apply to various territories. In the US there are ratings that allow graphic sex and violence but they are generally avoided in favour of the more financially viable (and viewable) R-rating. It's often this version that is shipped to other countries. Restrictions are also applied, arguably more stringently, to imported films such as *Haute Tension* and *Braindead*, both of which were savagely cut to make them acceptable as R-rated films. In the UK, animal violence is prohibited by law and excised from prints. In Japan pubic hair is prohibited, but not sex or extreme violence. The Central Board of Film Certification in India removes anything deemed 'offensive' including nudity, graphic violence and political sensitivity. In France, films are not cut but they can receive prohibitively high classifications for violence or be banned on political grounds (*The Battle of Algiers*) while in Germany horror films are routinely cut or banned outright. The result is a world where anything goes and everything is denied. Somewhere.

'YOU CAN'T KILL THE BOOGEYMAN'[8] – REPETITION, REMAKES, RECYCLING AND REINVENTION

A prominent aspect of any genre film is the familiarity of the concept, the repetition of ideas that provide a short-hand for audience tastes. Cinema is a commercial artform and its success is measured in cold hard cash spent at the box office, so proven storylines inevitably generate imitations. Since the earliest days of cinema, popular films have spawned sequels to keep the audience coming back for more. Why bother creating something entirely new, and untested in the marketplace, when existing material featuring popular characters is already there? What is unusual about the horror genre is the sheer number of sequels that can be generated. Sure, *The Godfather* and *Pirates of the Caribbean* have had two sequels (and may yet go on to more) but that doesn't compete with seven *Halloween* sequels and a remake, nearly a dozen *Friday the 13th* films or the eighteen follow ups to *Troublesome Night*.

There are three elements to the horror franchise based around the popularity of the original film. The first is that of the sequel. If a film is popular, continue the story but make it bigger, louder and with more thrills. Film fans can spend many happy hours debating whether there is a sequel that is truly greater than the original film, but the studios will keep churning them out until the returns diminish. The 1980s were a strange time for cinema, suffering as a result of the popularity in video. However, horror films thrived, giving us more *Nightmare on Elm Street* films than was really necessary. Perhaps this was a reflection of the fact that cinemas are dark places away from the prying eyes of other family members... and a horror flick is an ideal date environment for teen couples.

The next is that of the reinvention. Although purists will argue that the original is always the better film, it nevertheless makes sound business sense to rejuvenate past successes. Horror films are most popular with 15-24 year olds, so if a story works, why not make it again, but update it for the next generation? A popular story can easily accommodate a reinvention every decade or so. The Universal monster movies of the 1930s (*Dracula*, *Frankenstein*) were remade by Hammer in the 1950s and 1960s. These monsters appeared yet again in big budget Hollywood productions in the early 1990s as well as in a number of TV incarnations in the interim. They remain popular today, but each becomes relevant to its contemporary audience. *Dracula*, for example, remains one of the most filmed books with key adaptations in 1922, 1931, 1958, 1970, two in 1979, 1992, 2000/1 and so on. Guy Maddin's remarkable *Dracula: Pages from a Virgin's Diary* even turned the novel into a ballet.

Finally there are remakes. Some of the top horror films of the 1970s – *Dawn of the Dead*, *The Texas Chain Saw Massacre*, *The Hills Have Eyes*, *Halloween* – now find themselves 'sexed-up' for a modern audience with state-of-the-art gore effects and pounding soundtracks. Things become increasingly confusing when these films spawn their own sequels: after all, the film that came after George A Romero's *Dawn of the Dead* (1978) was *Day of the Dead* (1985), not *Dawn of the*

Dead 2. Is *The Hills Have Eyes 2* (2007) a remake of *The Hills Have Eyes 2* (1985) or a sequel to *The Hills Have Eyes* (2006) which was a remake of *The Hills Have Eyes* (1977)? Does it matter?

An altogether more contentious area is the foreign remake. Many classic horror films that were popular in their native country have been remade by Hollywood to appeal to an English-speaking audience who either can't be bothered to read subtitles, are unaware of the original's existence or simply unable to see the original. The remake becomes more bizarre when the directors who gained acclaim for their films remake them for the (richer) Hollywood studios – George Sluizer remade his excellent *Spoorloos* as the depressingly poor *The Vanishing* while Ole Bornedal was persuaded to remake his serial killer film *Nattevagten* as the less tense *Nightwatch*. Stranger still is the case of Hideo Nakata whose *Ringu* (1998), itself a remake of a 1995 TV movie but which gained international attention, was remade by Gore Verbinski in the States. For the sequel to the US film they brought in Nakata, who had helmed *Ringu 2* (1999) in Japan, to make *Ring 2* in Hollywood – but a different *Ring 2* to his Japanese sequel!

Audience turnover combined with the joy of the familiar has ensured that we will continue to get repetition, remakes and reinvention. From a marketing point of view, even if the audience has not seen the original film, the familiarity of the titles and characters means that half the advertising task – awareness of product – is already complete. The title '*Jaws*' alone is enough for most people to be aware of a killer shark movie because of cultural exposure to the iconic original. The title '*Tongue*', an imaginary film about ruthless mutant gila monsters terrorising Surrey, has no such association and would be far harder to market, even if it was a better product.

HORROR IN EUROPE

Europe has always been in turmoil, a collection of tribes and civilisations rising, falling, fighting, absorbing for thousands of years. It's a melange of cultures with different customs and beliefs but all at some point affected by the others. The oral, written and historical tales of the continent feed into the films it produces. Europe's history has given us gladiatorial bloodshed lit by night with human torches, genocide, pandemics, religious persecution, the Inquisition, torture and slavery. Greek legends, Icelandic epics, *Beowulf* and the literature of Webster, Goethe and de Sade have all fed into the wider cultural absorption of the horror genre. The *Malleus Maleficarum* was responsible for the torture and execution of thousands. The Crusades decimated the Middle East. In many ways the Europeans conceptually invented the horror film through folklore, literature and real life long before they had the means to realise it. All European countries have a film tradition, all have made horror films, but some countries have developed defined horror movements, while others have singular entries or filmmakers that have made their mark.

In Denmark, Benjamin Christensen's long gestating *Haxan* (1922) proved to be a revolutionary mixture of documentary, fantasy and reconstruction that is astonishing, even today, with its heady brew of demonic imagery, animation and scale. Christensen briefly moved to America, making a number of elaborate fantasy horror comedies before returning to Denmark. Denmark has a tradition of horror films from Dreyer's *Leaves From Satan's Book* (1919) to Martin Schmidt's bizarre *Sidste time* (1995), where a group of misbehaving students are picked off in after-school detention, and events outside the classroom, depicted on their televisions, clash with what they think they see. Maverick film-maker Lars von Trier's early *Epidemic* (1987) indicated that the director was more than capable of delivering the goods when it came to horror but it was the groundbreaking television series *Riget* (*The Kingdom,* 1994) and its sequel that really shone. The Kingdom Hospital is built on an ancient burial ground where the long dead still exert influence over the living. Its mixture of *Twin Peaks* style soap opera with outright horror – brain surgery without anaesthetic, zombies, body parts in fridges, ghosts in the escalator – marks it out as one of the more outrageous series ever made. With its Dane-hating Swedish surgeon Krogshøj and the ghost-sensitive patient Mrs Drusse adding to the humour, it's up to genre favourite Udo Kier to provide the series with its most bizarre moments, appearing as a giant mutant baby. Krogshøj must certainly find the blood and guts disturbing, as Sweden's very strict censorship of violence resulted in, until recently, very few examples of the genre outside the grim art-shock of Bergman's more extreme films.

Belgian director Harry Kümel's *Les rouges aux lèvres* (*Daughters of Darkness*, 1971) remains, arguably, the finest vampire film ever made, a ravishing and sensual experience. His *Malpertuis: Histoire d'une maison maudite* (1971) is an even more surreal example of the genre, where prisoners in a doomed mansion are bound by an oath kept from beyond the grave. Kümel's visual lyricism gives his films a dreamlike air but sadly most of his work after this period is unavailable for viewing. The Netherlands has recently seen a spate of horror films, revitalising a scant genre that includes George Sluizer's brilliantly disturbing *Spoorloos* (1988) and the enjoyable *De Lift* (1983), which, despite the seemingly unterrifying premise of a killer lift, manages to provide plenty of tension and scares. Director Dick Maas went on to make the gruesomely excel-lent action film *Amsterdamned* (1988) and a series of television come-dies, but always returned to the sick vein of black humour that typified *De Lift*, even managing to make a semi-sequel *Down* (2001) in America. More recently, Belgium's *The Ordeal* (2004) showed that it wasn't just

American films like *Hostel* (2005) that could be a gruelling exercise in torture and pain.

The now lost *Alraune* (1918) was an early example from Austria and Hungary featuring a mad scientist who fathers a demonic child by forcing a prostitute to mate with a mandrake root. Its director, Michael Curtiz, would later find fame in the US with another mad scientist film, *Dr X* (1932), and *The Walking Dead* (1936). And *Casablanca* (1943). In Turkey, *Dracula Istanbulda* (1953) was the first of many vampire films made in the country, while in Russia, vampires, and indeed all manner of supernatural beings, battled it out in the exhilarating *Nochnoy dozor* (*Night Watch,* 2004). The notorious Greek shocker *Ta Paidia tou diabolou* (*Island of Death*, 1972) launched first-time director Nico Mastorakis onto the world stage and he has continually, if sporadically, found work in the genre since. Widely banned and cut to ribbons in the UK, the film follows a warped couple killing any 'perverts' they find on a picturesque Greek island, although the definition seems a bit rich coming from someone who rapes a goat, drowns someone by forcing paint down their throat and harpoons rapacious hippies. Poland's visionary director Andrzej Zulawski gave us the 'Cthuluesque-tenticular-sex as relationship breakdown' surrealist masterpiece *Possession* (1981). More surrealism came from the master of animation Jan Svankmajer, the Czechoslovakian director of disturbing films such as *Muzné hry* (*Virile Games,* 1988), a criticism of football violence where two teams of the same man brutally kill each other in increasingly graphic and unusual ways – driving a train through a head or mutilating faces with bottles – as well as a number of Edgar Allan Poe adaptations.

British Horror Cinema

That British cinema has a long history of horror filmmaking should come as no surprise, and follows naturally from a heritage of imaginative literature that runs the gamut of quality from the heights of Shelley to the weekly Penny Dreadfuls that so outraged middle-class Victorian society even as they were eagerly devoured by the newly literate working classes. Early British horror films tended to appear on the bottom half of double bills or as shorts or serials. There were versions of the Dreadfuls such as *Sweeney Todd* (1926 and 1928), which, like their literary equivalents, rubbed shoulders with more respectable, but no less horrific, thrillers such as *The Lodger* (1927 and 1932). It was the success of the Universal films from America that really kickstarted the horror industry in the UK; a common language meant that Hollywood films were accessible and popular with British audiences in the early days of the talkies. Gaumont recognised the market pull of star power and hired (English) actor Boris Karloff, hot from his roles in *Frankenstein* (1931) and *The Mummy* (1932) to make *The Ghoul* (1933), a rancid portrayal of bitterness and greed whose foetid air makes for serious viewing, offset by the addition of a comedy character who goes some way towards lightening the tone. Professor Morlant is an archaeologist so convinced he has discovered the secret to eternal life he has arranged to be interred in a mausoleum from which he can rise from the dead. He bandages into his hand the life-awakening jewel necessary for the ancient spell to cheat death. He returns from the dead (although his gaunt corpse-like features were the wrong side of living when he was alive) a violent, superhuman killer. The film's financial success led to other productions with Universal's stars including Karloff in *The Man Who Changed His Mind* (1936) and Bela Lugosi in *Dark Eyes of London* (1940). However, the cost of these productions was prohibitive for many studios. What Britain needed was a star of its own. That star was Tod Slaughter – real name Norman Carter Slaughter.

Horror is a genre that paradoxically thrives in times of depression and war – like comedy, it is comfortingly cathartic. Slaughter was the face of British horror throughout the war years in a series of melodramatic fright pictures that drew on everything from true crime, the Penny Dreadfuls and even the works of Wilkie Collins. The Newcastle-born actor had presented his towering frame in a number of highly successful music hall horror shows so it seemed only natural to bring his talent to a wider audience. However, the resulting films were significantly less explicit than his stage work because of the censorship board. They nevertheless provided lucrative fare in such pictures as *Murder in the Red Barn* (1935) and his most famous role as *Sweeney Todd, The Demon Barber of Fleet Street* (1936) – the notorious British character of the macabre. Todd shaves so close that he slices his customers' arteries right open, dispatching their corpses in the basement where they can be stripped of cash, their butchered flesh the vital ingredient in the adjacent baker's famous pies. Despite numerous film and stage versions before and since – including a Sondheim musical filmed by Tim Burton and countless television adaptations – the part is Slaughter's own. Even bereft of the copious blood he employed in his stage version, he still strikes the viewer as a brutal and disturbing individual. Post-war, horror output was generally sparse and at the low end of the budget spectrum, filling in the lesser halves of double bills as 'quota quickies'. Ealing Studios' eventually influential anthology *Dead of Night* (1945) provided a rare highpoint in Britain's horror output of the period but it would be some time before a definitive movement would emerge. When it did, though, it created a brand that is still recognised the world over as synonymous with the genre.

Hammer films had, under various names, been running since the mid-1930s. Although there were some borderline genre films in its early incarnation – including Bela Lugosi in *The Mystery of the Marie Celeste* (1936) – the studio was best known for producing adaptations of popular radio and television shows. Pivotal to their development was a relatively large-budget distillation of the BBC's *Quatermass Experiment*, Nigel Kneale's terrifying six-part serial. Hammer slimmed down the screenplay and renamed the film *The Quatermass Xperiment* (1955) to emphasise the X-rated nature of the film. It was a huge success despite its certificate, which restricted screenings to certain cinema chains only. The revenue gained meant that the company could move to colour film stock and embark upon what was to be their most ambitious project yet – *The Curse of Frankenstein* (1957). Unable to utilise Jack Pierce's iconic design for Karloff's flat-headed version of the monster, Hammer approached the creature's design as one of decomposing, flaccid, crudely stitched flesh. The horrific monster was inhabited with sympathetic yet primal ferocity by the towering frame of Christopher Lee. His creator, Baron Frankenstein, was played by the gaunt yet athletic Peter Cushing, relishing his part told in flashback from the prison cell where he awaits execution. It's a taut, operatic tragedy played with vitality and gusto. It was quite unlike anything the normally reserved (Powell and Pressburger excepted) British film industry had produced – blisteringly paced and luridly coloured. It was box office dynamite. The pair returned, along with director Terence Fisher, in the similarly energetic *Dracula* (aka *The Horror of Dracula*, 1958), confirming Hammer's place as the face of world horror. And so the company, which still continued producing non-genre films alongside its more celebrated output, became the first since Universal (with whom they made a lucrative deal to reinterpret many of their horror classics following these successes) to be accepted globally.

For the next 15 years they would produce a consistently well-received body of work. This included *Curse of the Werewolf* (1961), vampire films (*Twins of Evil* [1971], *Vampire Circus* [1971]), psychological thrillers (*Nanny* [1965], *Paranoiac* [1963]), Satanist pictures (*The Devil Rides Out* [1968]), literary adaptations such as *Hound of the Baskervilles* (1959) and *Phantom of the Opera* (1962), as well as expanding the *Dracula* and *Frankenstein* franchises. But eventually the social climate of the 1970s put an end to the company's cinematic ambitions. They had difficulty adapting to the changing times, and with America producing heartfelt contemporary horror, which was grimy and sleazy, Hammer's period pieces, despite the addition of nudity and more gore, seemed too quaint. Attempts to revitalise the company with contemporary spins on familiar tales, *Dracula AD1972* for example, were box office disappointments, the company remaining afloat through cheap comedy spin-offs of domestic television comedies. Their final feature *To the Devil a Daughter* was released in 1976, cashing in on the demonic kid boom.

During Hammer's golden period other companies sought a piece of

Britain's horror pie. Most successful was Amicus, fronted by Milton Subotsky. Among the better productions to come from Amicus were a series of portmanteau films; their standalone features were generally inferior. *Dr Terror's House of Horrors* (1965) marked their first foray into the format, with Peter Cushing as the sinister Dr Schreck, telling the fortunes of five doomed passengers on a train. The tales involve vampires, werewolves and, that perennial horror favourite, the animated severed hand. A large number of cast and crew from the Hammer stable would be involved in these productions although the heads of the two companies were bitter rivals. Later films expanded the basic premise, with *Tales from the Crypt* (1972) and *Vault of Horror* (1973) being adapted from the EC Horror comics of the same name. Amicus productions never tried to outdo Hammer in the sex and violence stakes and have a more fantastical or phantasmagorical feel to them than the full-bloodied myth-making of Hammer's best. They, too, struggled as the 1970s progressed, even jumping on the trendy bandwagon with the ill-advised werewolf mystery (complete with a self-imposed break before the beast's identity is revealed so that audiences could see if they got it right) *The Beast Must Die* (1974). This lame dog of a film saw Subotsky scamper back to familiar portmanteau territory for the hilarious killer cat anthology *The Uncanny* (1977) and the kid-friendly *The Monster Club* (1980).

If Amicus were filling a fantastical part of the market without Hammer's visceral grue then other companies with rather less cash in their coffers were happy to try and fill a market gap. Tigon Films may have produced pictures of varying quality but Michael Reeves was definitely one of their better directors. The mind-bending psychedelic horror *The Sorcerers* (1967), with Boris Karloff, tapped into the dark underbelly of 1960s Britain in a disorientating and disturbing manner, but it was his masterpiece (and final film, he died tragically young) *Witchfinder General* (1968) that really had an impact. Reeves' tale of Matthew Hopkins' campaign of terror, burning countless women in the name of religion to further his financial and sexual appetites, may have taken liberties with historical fact but made for compellingly dark viewing. There is no fantasy respite here and ultimately no heroes. When Ian Ogilvy finally dismembers Vincent Price's evil witchfinder (in a rare role totally devoid of Price's usual camp overtones) the camera shows us that, after all the rape and killing, he has gone completely mad. There is no room for cosy endings in Reeves' bleak but engaging film. Tigon Films slipped out of the horror market in the 1970s but their place was filled with opportunistic independent entrepreneurs with a love of film and an eye on the X-rated market. With world cinema in a state of rebellion these filmmakers pushed the boundaries of what was acceptable on the big screen. Peter Walker gave us, among others, *The House of Whipcord* (1974), a very British take on underground justice mixed with mild S&M imagery, and the delirious mother and daughter killers film *Frightmare* (1974) with its groundbreaking use of household tools – most famously an electric drill – as a way of dispatching unfortunates. Norman J Warren gave us the delights of *Satan's Slave* (1976), *Prey* (1977) and the *Alien* (1979) homage, the gloriously offensively titled alien rape film *Inseminoid* (1980). Like many of the time Warren filled his films with both sex and violence. Aware that the BBFC were occasionally erratic in their approach to censorship, this allowed him to release different versions of the film to appeal to different markets – more sex in the European prints and more gore in the American and Japanese versions.

Regardless of the pioneering spirit and the punk DIY ethic there was little doubt that the British film industry in general was not living up to its 1960s heyday. Horror films became more sporadic and eventually seemed to fizzle out entirely for a while. There were exceptions of course. Ridley Scott's *Alien* used its science fiction MacGuffin to wrong-foot its audience, making the scares all the more horrific and unexpected. A deliberately languid first half eventually establishes that a dead alien lifeform is aboard the Nostromo, a commercial spaceship. But is it really dead? Crew member Kane suddenly starts having violent spasms at the meal table. A gestating alien, lodged inside him, erupts from his chest, showering his distraught colleagues with blood and flesh. The mewling creature darts off only to grow rapidly and pick off the crew one by one. *Alien*'s revolutionary use of design, the harsh minimalist spaceship contrasting with the nightmarishly organic worlds of HR Giger, created a claustrophobic environment that bettered any contemporary slasher. Almost diametrically opposed was Neil Jordan's ravishing Angela Carter adaptation *The Company of Wolves* (1984), a portmanteau film connecting lycanthropy with sexual awakening. The fairytale worlds are Grimm indeed, where little girls are certainly not safe wandering the forests alone. Jordan's fantasy worlds feature painful transformations from man to beast including a remarkable scene where a wolf literally sheds its human skin by emerging from a man's mouth, orgies of glutinous shapeshifters and rottenness beneath the surface of respectable wedlock. *The Company of Wolves* was released in 1984, the year everything changed.

The video recorder had created a boom industry in rental tapes but the big studios had been slow to cash in. The market was wide open for smaller companies to make a mark, which they did by releasing a slew of cheaply produced animations, soft-core pornography and horror films. Because the censors only viewed cinematic releases these tapes were not required to go through the certification process. Although many companies released tapes cut in line with their cinema releases some did not and others released films highly unlikely to gain certification. The tabloid newspapers, spurred by the upturn in Thatcher-Reagan puritanism, declared these to be 'Video Nasties' that corrupted the young. Video companies and retailers were prosecuted, films banned and a regime instigated whereby video cassettes would be subject to even more ruthless censorship than their celluloid counterparts. True, many of the films banned were either bad or downright tasteless (*Gestapo's Last Orgy* [1977]) but that was not the point. The principle of free expression had been curtailed, and for the next 16 years Britain would suffer the heaviest censorship system in the western world. Among those considered unsuitable were future *Spider-Man* (2002) director Sam Raimi's superb splatter comedy *The Evil Dead* (1982), Dario Argento's operatic and stylish *Inferno* (1980) and even the arthouse marriage breakdown horror (albeit with fleshy tenticular mutant alien sex) *Possession* (1981). The effect on the UK horror scene was devastating. Although Palace Pictures produced *Dream Demon* (1987) and Working Title the occasionally surreal *Paperhouse* (1988), the damage had been done and further productions were sporadic.

Clive Barker's feature debut *Hellraiser* (1987) told a tight tale of sado-masochism and resurrection, creating the enduring icon of Pinhead (unnamed in the original film) with his old friend Doug Bradley. *Hellraiser* raised the stakes in terms of prosthetic effects technology as pain-loving Frank is agonisingly resurrected from the blood of slaughtered businessmen seeking cheap sex with his accomplice lover. Richard Stanley was one of the more exciting directors at the time. *Hardware* (1990) depicted a bleak post-apocalyptic future. A man discovers a robot's head in the desert and brings it back to his girlfriend, whereupon it wreaks bloody havoc as it tries to reassemble itself. Stanley followed this with the remarkable *Dust Devil* (1992), the filming of which was almost as frightening as the finished result, if his diaries are anything to go by. Stanley's success led him to Hollywood to film his dream project – *The Island of Dr Moreau* (1996) – but he was fired after only four days. Allegedly he turned up on set in full monster costume to keep tabs on the production. And then, bar the odd spirited attempt such as Ken Russell's deranged camp classic *The Lair of the White Worm* (1988), with its more-is-more ethic and outrageous digital imagery, and the comedy *I Bought a Vampire Motorcycle* (1990), the British horror film pretty much died off...

...only to rise once more from its putrid grave a decade later. Changes in the board at the BBFC, the emergence of new filmmakers and a ruling from the EU that made the extremes of British censorship untenable (although many films are still routinely censored, sometimes to get lower classifications), saw the possibilities of home-produced horror emerge once more. *Deathwatch* (2002) moved the ghost story to the already scary setting of the World War I trenches. *My Little Eye* (2002) used its low budget effectively by making video a necessary part of the aesthetic in a cross between the popular TV gawp-show *Big Brother* and any number of giallo. Werewolves returned once more in *Dog Soldiers* (2002), a darkly comic horror. Director Neil Marshall followed this impressive debut feature with the pot-holing terror of *The Descent* (2005), in which a group of women get stuck in a cave system and find themselves facing the triple adversity of their environment, each other and a group of cannibalistic underground dwellers. The tension is as razor sharp as their adversaries' teeth. Effective use of sound – the slow drips of water punctuated by inhuman screeches – makes for consistently jittery viewing. The rise in horror filmmaking in the UK has even led to more knowingly comic fare such as *Shaun of the Dead* (2005), Jake West's reprehensibly enjoyable *Evil Aliens* (2006) and the team-bonding-exercise-gone-wrong slasher film *Severance* (2006). Indeed the relaxation in censorship has resulted in many British cinemas showing films that would be deemed unsuitable as an R-rating in the US. How times have changed.

Italian Horror Cinema

Italy was arguably at the forefront of developing cinema as a spectacular, narrative-based artform, producing lavish epics at a time when other countries were still churning out shorts and trick films. A speciality of early Italian cinema was the historical epic, such as the downfall of Pompeii, which offered filmmakers the opportunity to revel in scenes of debauchery and the divine retribution of violence inflicted on 'wicked' people. *Quo Vadis* (1912) was the first film to feature custom-built sets, creating a worldwide sensation and a demand for Italian set designers, craftsmen and art directors that continues to this day. Overall, they had style. Scenes of violence and decadence were allowed because the epics were either educational or fulfilled some moral need – you couldn't, the argument went, condemn sin without seeing what sin was. It was a trick Hollywood would also adopt under increasingly harsh censorship regimes. With all the violence, as well as Italy's links to the fantastical through its past and the emphasis on suffering in Roman Catholicism, it is perhaps surprising that a horror movement took so long to emerge.

At Italian cinema's height of artistic achievement there was a crippling blow. Mussolini's fascists took hold of the country in 1922 and they established Cinecittà, still one of the world's most famous production studios. Following the downfall of Mussolini in 1943, a new wave of Italian cinema emerged, countering the bland fantasies of the fascist era, and emphasising realism. Though critically lauded it would be some time before Italian cinema would reclaim the flamboyance of its early years. By the 1960s a new confidence had returned and with it the historical epic (sword and sandal films), the aggressive 'spaghetti' westerns and a new wave of horror films, harking back to the stylish depiction of sex and violence that had made Italy so world renowned. This time it didn't have to be educational.

Riccardo Freda brought to life the lurid tale of a scientist who drains the blood of nubile women in *I Vampiri* (1956), the first of the new wave of Italian horror. The film was actually finished by a young Mario Bava who would go on to be instrumental in the rise of the horror film. Freda followed his success with the Mayan blob-monster film *Caltiki – il mostro immortale* (1959) before making a series of sword and sandal films, eventually merging the two genres for *Maciste all'inferno* (1962), a bizarre but entertaining fantasy where the hero has to travel through Hell to destroy a witch who has cursed the earth. His masterpiece came in the dark and influential shocker *L'Orribile segreto del Dr Hichcock* (1962), starring the undisputed queen of horror Barbara Steele. Sumptuously photographed in full colour widescreen, it tells the story of a nineteenth-century doctor who drugs his wife so he can fulfil his dark necrophilic needs in disturbing sexual role-plays. Although this is played discreetly, the film's subject matter remains taboo to this day, despite making for compelling and, at times, beautiful viewing. He continued to make films but only returned to true horror in his last picture, *Follia Omicida* (1981).

Freda provided the seeds for the new generation of horror film-makers, particularly Mario Bava, whose films were distinctively Italian, despite the presence of international stars, who were recruited to enhance sales overseas. Bava had followed his stunning debut *Black Sunday* (1960) with a series of fantasy films and *La Frusta e il corpo* (1963), a similar tale to *L'Orribile segreto del Dr Hichcock*. The true breakthrough came with *La Ragazza che sapeva troppo* (*The Girl Who Knew Too Much*,1963) and *Sei donne per l'assassino* (*Blood and Black Lace,* 1964), films that launched not just imitators but an entire genre. Bava took the horror film away from its classic literary past and brought it into the contemporary world. Giallo are a form of distinctive pulp crime novels that get their name from their yellow covers, covers offering sala-cious stories, titillation and violence. It was a term that would define a new genre of film, where killers murder their victims in an elaborate fashion and the origins of their crimes are revealed by increasingly convoluted means. The giallo's main calling card is style – ravishing camerawork, intricate design, bloody killings, an unknown killer of inde-terminate sex, beautiful women, operatic flourishes – like *Grand Guignol* Agatha Christie filmed in a fashion house. *Blood and Black Lace* provided the blueprint for all subsequent giallo. It would take some years for the genre really to take hold, starting with Dario Argento's *Bird with the Crystal Plumage* (1970) and dominating the scene until the mid-1970s – although even then the genre didn't die out, but merely slowed down. Key directors included Aldo Lado (*Who Saw Her Die?* [1972], *Short Night of the Glass Dolls* [1971]), Massimo Dallamano (*What Have You Done to Solange?* [1972], featuring a murderer at large in a girls' school who kills using a knife as a sexual substitute) and Sergio Martino (*I corpi presen-tano tracce di violenza carnale* [*Torso*, 1973], an often heavily censored film about the strangulation of beautiful college students). Giallo continues to be made to this day with films such as Argento's *Non ho sonno* (*Sleepless*, 2001). The influence of the giallo on the slasher film, not to mention the modern thriller (*Kiss the Girls* [1997], *Se7en* [1995]), cannot be overestimated.

The giallo had a sense of literary (albeit pulp) validity but as the 1970s progressed the decade's legendary drive to excess, to hedonistic nihilism, was beginning to take hold and, rather than contrast exploitation with style, why not just go for the exploitation? Although there are many examples of exemplary filmmaking during this period, there was a perceived drive to up the ante in terms of stomach-churning grue and sexualised violence. This marked the Italian 'nasty' era – a term derived from their almost universal purging from the UK's video shelves – that made the films controversial the world over. Not all of the films were based on indigenous genres; many derived from external sources, as had previously occured with the reinvention of the American western in the 1960s. Liliana Cavani's *The Night Porter* (1974) was an arthouse success tackling a controversial post-war sado-masochistic relationship between a concentration camp officer (Dirk Bogarde) and an ex-inmate (Charlotte Rampling), similar in tone to Luchino Visconti's earlier Nazi film *The Damned* (1969). The films in their wake, however, took more of a cue from *Love Camp No 7* (1969, Australia, released 1974), launching a series of 'Nasty Nazi' exploitation flicks of staggering insensitivity and offensiveness. Although there is plenty of uneasy artistic merit in Tinto Brass's epically designed *Salon Kitty* (1976) the exploitation is kept predominantly within a brothel. *Gestapo's Last Orgy* (1977) and *La Bestia in calore* (1977) are far more difficult films to take, the latter's extremely graphic torture scenes only offset by the sheer stupidity of the central premise – a kind of rapacious Frankenstein's monster beast with a taste for flesh and pubic hair – and the mercifully unrealistic concentration camp settings.

However, many of these films would further obliterate good taste by including brief insertions of genuine atrocities. The use of documentary footage had a basis in Italian cinema's past with the hugely influential shockumentary *Mondo Cane* (1962), a series of grotesque rituals and cruelties, marketed as educational but basically containing unrelated clips of shocking footage paraded as anthropology. Its success – although *Mondo Cane* is a serious film, the use of real death footage and, in later films, of faked footage treated as real – spawned a number of sequels and spin-offs that continue to this day, including the notorious but serious *Africa Addido* (1966), a 140-minute catalogue of African tribal slaughter and animal abuse. The Mondo film's aesthetic, its fascinated but xenophobic attitude to tribalism and its emphasis on animal atrocities fed directly into another notorious Italian genre – the cannibal film. Ruggero Deodato made his first cannibal film in 1977, *Ultimo Mondo Cannibale*, specifically invoking the legacy of *Mondo Cane* (despite its entirely fictional premise), set in a remote South East Asian island where a small group of rich westerners stumble into a tribe of cannibals. The same year saw exploitation regular Joe D'Amato produce *Emanuelle e gli Ultimi Cannibali* (*Emmanuel and the Last Cannibals*). Three years later Deodato would shock the authorities and the world with *Cannibal Holocaust* (1980). The story follows a group of anthropologists seeking the whereabouts of a missing crew who had been filming a documentary about cannibal tribes in the rainforests. After witnessing a number of disturbing events they finally manage to obtain the crew's footage from one of the tribes, only to be shocked by what they discover. The clever use of a 'film within a film' questions the nature of watching (and faking) shockumentaries and the sense of realism gained by verité-style footage pre-dates *The Blair Witch Project* (1999) by two decades. It is the nature of the material that is the root of the film's controversy – indeed the Italian authorities impounded it believing it to be a genuine snuff film. It contains scenes of gang rape, executions, a woman wholly impaled on a stake, eviscerations, castrations, immolations and finally cannibalism. Further linking the film to the Mondo cycle was the inclusion of several scenes of animal cruelty shot specifically for the film, much to the disgust of some of those who were involved and ensuring that the film would never be passed uncut in the UK. The brief period *Cannibal Holocaust* was on Italian screens brought in so much money that a slew of films followed including *Mondo Cannibale* (1980), *Apocalisse Domani* (1980) and two from the original cannibal film director Umberto Lenzi – *Mangiati Vivi* (*Eaten Alive*, 1980) and *Cannibal*

Ferox (1981). Lenzi had previously made the film *Deep River Savages* in 1972.

The success of *Dawn of the Dead* (1978) launched a slew of Italian homages, although they generally adopted more exotic locales than Romero's claustrophobic consumerist hell. Though controversial, they never quite gained the heights of hysteria of the cannibal films, as they were clearly grounded in fantasy. It's far easier to accept cannibalism by the reanimated dead than entertain the prospect of a real person chomping down on someone. This small genre peaked with the work of Lucio Fulci but there were other films of merit, most notably Umberto Lenzi's *Incubo sulla città contaminata* (*Nightmare City*, 1980) which bucked the trend for the slow-moving dead, a trait that would briefly return in moments of Zack Snyder's American *Dawn of the Dead* (2004) remake.

By the mid-1980s, trends had moved on. Lamberto (son of Mario) Bava emerged as a sporadic talent. Starting with proto-giallo *Macabro* (1980) and *La Casa con la scala nel buio* (*A Blade in the Dark*, 1983), he continues to make genre films to this day (*The Torturer*, 2005). His finest moment came with the first of the films he made in the *Demons* series. *Dèmoni* (1985) is a wild, exhilarating pop-splatter film of the highest order. A group of young people end up being trapped in a cinema showing a preview of a new horror film, initially unaware that their numbers are being diminished, turned into ravaging puss-spewing demons. What marks *Dèmoni* out is the apparently endless series of surprises the film has to offer – a postmodern film within a film relating to events the kids are watching, ushers dressed as demons promoting the film becoming actual demons, unusual make-up effects, plenty of green gore and any number of gruesome killings. Just when you think the combination of disco splatter can't get any better a helicopter conveniently (and impressively) crashes into the cinema and the hero goes on a mass chopping spree with a handy samurai sword. The pleasingly loud soundtrack just adds to the gruesome *joie de vivre* and it exudes genre awareness years before *Scream* (1996). The sequel, in which a witch emerges from a TV, *Videodrome*-style, and terrorises an apartment block is enjoyable but never quite reaches the level of hysteria that the first film manages.

One of Dario Argento's protégés, Michele Soavi, emerged as a promising talent with a strong sense of visual style and humour. His debut giallo *Deliria* (*Stagefright*, 1984) featured a killer disguised as an owl butchering a troupe of actors, including the memorable scene where cast members are attacked with an axe that still has the previous wielder's arm attached to it. If his next films *La Chiesa* (1989) and *La Setta* (1991) were overly marketed as producer Argento's, they were nevertheless notable for their striking visualisations of hell on earth. To date his last completed feature was *Dellamorte Dellamore* (1994) although he has continued to work in television.

The Italian tradition of creating stylish and elaborate tableaux of sex and violence has produced some of the horror genre's most distinctive, and at times controversial, films. The combination of art and exploitation has made the films of its golden years (from 1960 to 1980) among the most sustained and fruitful in the genre, ranging from the pinnacles of technical artistry to the barrel-scraping bottoms of exploitation's most shameful moments.

French Horror Cinema

France cannot only be credited with the invention of cinema, but also the earliest horror film. While the realist works of the Lumière brothers had audiences fleeing from the cinema in terror at the image of an approaching train arriving at a railway station, one of their earliest audience members was inspired to develop a whole new approach to the cinematic form – the artistic urge to create, not document. Georges Méliès was cinema's premier magician – an illusionist who recognised the potential of cinema to create trick photography and special effects, a 'créateur du spectacle cinématographique'. In a series of fantasies and even historical recreations he used the manipulative power of film to show faked beheadings, a man whose head is pumped up like a balloon until it pops and magical journeys to the moon or beneath the Channel. On Christmas Eve, 1896, he unveiled *Le Manoir du diable*, a two-minute film that features a bat changing into Mephistopheles and familiar horror film trappings such as witches, bubbling cauldrons and skeletons. Although intended as an amusing Christmas novelty, the elements of the horror film can be traced to this short in its adoption of the macabre and fantastic. Many other films followed, including *Le chaudron infernal* (1903), where two devils create spirits by throwing women in a burning cauldron, *Le Monstre* (1903), featuring a reanimated skeleton under the gaze of the Sphinx whose neck can elongate in terrifying fashion and *Le diable noir* (1905), where an acrobatic imp causes mayhem and mischief in the room of an unfortunate gentleman. Devils crop up in a number of his films, as do witches, imps, demons, skeletons and sorcerers. However, despite Méliès' imagination and still-inspiring effects work – see him chastising increasing numbers of his own disembodied head in *Un homme de têtes* (1898) for a wonderful example – his films became seen as nothing more than archaic novelties as cinema strove to find ways of expressing more complex narratives and developing a language of images to convey them.

An early admirer of Méliès was Louis Feuillade who began directing trick pictures in a similar manner before producing a bewildering number of films (over 600) in genres as diverse as the biblical epic, realist docudramas and child comedy films. Feuillade progressed to make more narratively complex pieces and serial works designed to keep audiences returning to the cinema. His early triumph *Fantômas* (1913) has as the titular character an arch-criminal mastermind who terrorises Paris with increasingly devious and elaborate plans – drugs, poisonings, kidnapping, orgies and even a story where Fantômas disguises the perpetrator of the crime by wearing the skin peeled from a dead man's hands to fake the fingerprints. The character was so popular that five luridly melodramatic serials were made. In Feuillade's nightmarish landscape anything is possible, proving to be influential on both the Surrealist movement and upon future makers of thrillers such as Hitchcock and Fritz Lang.

What is interesting is that Feuillade uses carefully constructed tableau framing to allow the viewer into his story and freeform editing between lengthy, artistically composed shots. This use of cinematic language would eventually be supplanted by the classical Hollywood style perfected by DW Griffith, but Feuillade's alternative approach to film language would see later adopters in the shape of Jean-Luc Godard, Jean Rollin and Britain's Peter Greenaway. In 1915, Feuillade gave the screen its first memorable female villain. In *Les Vampires* the sleek, slinky, black-clad figure of Irma Vep (anagram fans need little help here), played with kohl-eyed intensity by Musidora, planning her diabolically evil plans from her chaise longue, again proved that the villains of the piece were far more interesting than the authorities that chased them. Unfortunately for Feuillade the real authorities also spotted this and his films came under scrutiny for their excessive and immoral depictions of violence, criminal behaviour and their implication that high society was a hotbed of lasciviousness. It meant that Feuillade's later films would have to give more credence to the side of the law rather than sensationalising the villain. In many ways it stifled further growth of the French horror film, to the extent that horror films made in France by non-French directors, such as Carl Dreyer's *Vampyr* (1932), would be treated with disdain and derision. The toil of two world wars and a tendency for French cinema to entrench into either sophisticated counter-Hollywood art films or play-to-the-stalls farces meant that little outside the critical or commercially successful genres received much attention.

France never really developed a horror movement to the extent that, say, Britain or Italy did, but there were a number of auteurs whose distinctive approach to the genre led to some wonderful films that were unconventional in execution. Screenwriter-turned-director Henri-Georges Clouzot was instrumental in bringing a harder pulp edge to French cinema with a series of murder mysteries and crime thrillers. His *Le Salaire de la peur* (*Wages of Fear,* 1953) remains one of the most tense and exacting films ever made. He put these skills to great effect in *Les Diaboliques* (1955), a lurid thriller notable for refining the idea of cinematic shock to a fine art. No longer would horror be limited to thematic elements such as the supernatural or gruesome murder but also stylistic ones such as the sudden scare and the need to affect an audience physically. The influence of *Les Diaboliques* on the technique of the horror film cannot be overestimated. However, the film's reliance on real-world explanations meant that for French cinema the use of suspense, tension and sudden shock would be more associated with the thriller (such as the oeuvre of Claude Chabrol) than with the horror per se.

Georges Franju was a cinephile who, with Henri Langlois, founded the Cinémathèque Française, France's most important film archive. He was best known as an archivist but also made films, such as *Le sang des bêtes* (1949), a still-shocking but poetic documentary about practices at a French abattoir. *Les yeux sans visage* (1959) remains his masterpiece with its tragic yet beautiful story, elegiacally portrayed in trails of light and blood. Again the film would prove influential in a number of ways – it reintroduced the idea of the 'arthouse horror', an apparently oxymoronic term in the eyes of many, but it also heralded an emphasis on the viscera of horror, of immersion into the actualities of blood and gore, that almost goaded the audience into turning away.

There was one man, however, whose unique vision has made him France's most consistent horror auteur for 40 years – Jean Rollin. Rollin's eccentric and beguiling output of horror films are among the most striking of low-budget cinema, but remain highly divisive – detractors bemoan incoherent plotting, slow pacing and borderline pornography while adherents laud his films' poetic lyricism, surrealism and ambiguous territories pitched between pain and eroticism. The most common adversaries in his films are vampires but often they are figures of sympathy as well as fear – populating a world pitched between European underground comic books and poetry, between high art (René Magritte, Paul Delvaux) and pulp melodrama. Rollin's first feature, an audacious mixture of S&M pulp and delirious narrative conceit (originally a 45-minute film, the characters who die at the end of the first half are resurrected for the second half) *Le viol du vampire* shocked audiences at the height of the May 1968 student riots in Paris with its unconventional approach to filmmaking. His second feature *La vampire nue* (1970) was an eye-searingly colourful, Sadean science-fiction story featuring a vampire race determined to return to their home planet while *Le frisson des vampires'* (1971) use of disorientating rock music and non-diegetic foley contrasted striking scenes of naked vampires emerging from grandfather clocks at the stroke of midnight. *Requiem pour un vampire* (1971) is a bewitching amalgam of knowingly artistic compositions juxtaposed with scenes of sadomasochistic sex and torture. Others include the gloriously pulpy *Les Démoniaques* (1974), *Les Raisins de la mort* (1978), *Fascination* (1979), the tragic *La Morte vivante* (1982), *Les Deux orphelines vampires* (1997) and *La Fiancée de Dracula* (2002).

Other genre films were few and far between. Bruno Gantillon's *Morgane et ses nymphes* (*Slave Girls of Morgana Le Fey,* 1971) is a Rollinesque fantasy set in a castle in rural France where Morgane offers her captives eternal beauty or a life decaying in her dungeons. Elegant use of lighting and smoke create an atmospheric fable akin to a modern day fairy tale. *Il Etait une fois, le diable* (1986) features a rampaging mutant soldier ripping the throats and entrails from local villagers, throwing in additional undead creatures when things start flagging. *La Revanche des mortes vivantes* (1987), directed by part-time pornographer Pierre Reinhard, is a 1970s exploitation flick that came a decade too late, clearly showing scant regard for continuity or women's clothing but having enough cheesy gross-out effects to get through its short running time.

France is now experiencing a new wave of horror film talent. A slew of arthouse shockers introduced a radical edge to French cinema that outraged cinemagoers, even as they flocked to see such turgid pornography as *Romance* (1999), the pretentious rape and violence nasty *Irréversible* (2002) and the hard-core and revenge killings film *Baise-moi* (2000). While these filmmakers were pushing the boundaries by justifying their work in terms of artistic merit others were making films without the need for protestation, producing films for entertainment. *Promenons-nous dans les bois* (*Deeper in the Woods,* 2000) is a well-mounted slasher cum giallo set in a remote country mansion where a group of actors are hired to entertain at a boy's birthday party. However, there is, inevitably, a serial killer on the loose and soon the bodies start mounting and the suspicions flying. Elements of horror creep into the works of Jean-Christophe Grangé, whose novels and screenplays have revitalised the hard crime drama, including two films in the *Les Rivières pourpres* (*Crimson River,* 2000) series and the slasher as crime film *L' Empire des loups* (*Empire of the Wolves,* 2005). *Le Pacte des loups* (*Brotherhood of the Wolf,* 2001) by Christophe Gans is an exhilarating blend of monster, martial arts and detective film set in eighteenth-century France. Grégoire de Fronsac and Mani are given the task of unearthing the savage beast that is eating villagers deep in the French countryside and includes some breathtaking first-person camerawork depicting the attacks which further raises the audience's expectation of the beast's eventual revelation. Gans had previously worked on the horror anthology *Necronomicon* (1994) as well as another genre twister *Crying Freeman* (1995). His latest film was a Hollywood adaptation of Japanese videogame franchise *Silent Hill* (2006), which Gans filled to the brim with disturbing, atmospheric but ultimately disassociated imagery including a tense navigation of a corridor filled with zombie nurses and a huge demon capable of skinning a man in one swipe.

Alexandre Aja's second feature *Haute tension* (2003), despite its restrictive N-17 rating, also resulted in a quick Stateside move to direct a similarly tense remake of *The Hills Have Eyes* (2006). These are symptomatic of the French horror film gaining confidence. *Ils* (2006) is a taut, tight movie set in Romania as French teacher Clementine and her partner Lucas find themselves trapped in their own home and hunted by figures who have presumably recently abducted a local mother and daughter. The tension is unbearable as they rush through the house – windows suddenly crash open, creaks and clicks surround them as they hide and tentative peeps through keyholes lead to very nasty consequences. Kim Chapiron's debut feature *Sheitan* (*Satan,* 2006) shows a lot of promise amidst the plethora of gross-out horror and attempts at teen comedy. Vincent Cassell gives a barnstorming performance as a Satan-worshipping shepherd intent on carrying out demonic rituals just as a bunch of teenage revellers come to town. Foul-mouthed and all-out grotesque, the sheer energy of *Sheitan* places it as pleasingly disreputable entertainment.

German Horror Cinema

Germany has a culture rich in folklore and fantasy, from the celebrated collections of the Brothers Grimm to the outlandish tales of Baron Münchhausen, mythical operas with dragons to slay, the poetic horrors of damnation in the works of Goethe and the fantastical tales of Heinrich Hoffmann. All have had a considerable influence on the nature of German cinema and in particular fantasy and horror films. Germany has a formidable reputation for its horror films but that reputation lies with a handful of influential works released in the early years of cinema. Germany's main studio Universum Film AG was populated by stars and directors – such as FW Murnau and Ernst Lubitsch – many of whom migrated from the theatre. The first bankable star of the silver screen was Paul Wegener who appeared as *The Student of Prague* (1913), a reworking of the Faust legend, selling his reflection to a magician in return for prosperity. It marked the start of a cycle of German macabre cinema that continued with Wegener in *Der Golem* (1915). This was the first of many adaptations of a Jewish legend about a towering clay creature brought to life to terrorise the locals, only to be placated by the most fragile of children, depicting innocence in the shadow of fear. Although *Der Golem* had a profound effect on the development of the horror film it is perhaps ironic that the two most iconic of the early horrors, *The Cabinet of Dr Caligari* (1919) and *Nosferatu, eine Symphonie des Grauens* (1921), were respectively derided and suppressed. Robert Weine's *The Cabinet of Dr Caligari* forced its expres-

The original Schreck. *Nosferatu.*

sionist sensibilities onto the screen to create a fragmented and distorted view of reality. Its visual and psychological impact is still being felt today, most notably in the works of Tim Burton. FW Murnau's *Nosferatu* had a similarly tortured fate. This low budget but highly impressive expressionist masterpiece has proved to be the blueprint for countless horrors in its use of creeping shadows, horrific make-up effects and macabre, almost fableistic, atmosphere. Although the film was a success, prints were ordered to be destroyed as Murnau had not obtained clearance from the widow of Bram Stoker to make what was clearly an adaptation of *Dracula.* This must have come as something of a shock to Murnau who had no such problem when making a version of *Jekyll and Hyde*, *Der Januskopf* (1920), a film which is now lost. Copyright and budget considerations were not an issue in *Faust* (1926), an astonishing flight of fantasy horror from the last years of Germany's golden age of film.

Mephistopheles takes Faust on a flight to tempt him into signing away his soul, showing him the heavens and the world's most beautiful woman in a breathtaking sequence of pure visual storytelling. Mephistopheles comes for the doomed Faust in the form of an angel turned devil, towering over the town like a mountain, his jet-black cloak engulfing the diminutive buildings in pure malevolent darkness as Faust cowers in abject fear. As with Fritz Lang's *Metropolis* (1927) and his two *Nibelungen* (1924) films this is an epic, lavish production. But outside of Germany's dream factory the Weimar Republic was beginning to see cracks. With the Great Depression came an economic crash in the US and Europe. Germany was hit particularly badly.

In the 1920s two notorious serial killers had made their mark in Germany: Fritz Haarmann, the 'Butcher of Hanover', and Peter Kürten, 'The Vampire of Düsseldorf'. The latter formed the basis for Fritz Lang's seminal shocker *M* (1931), starring Peter Lorre as Hans, an apparently genial man who befriends children in order to murder them. As the bodies mount up it's not only the police who want to find the killer but the criminal underground, who only want to be associated with 'good' crime, not implied paedophilia and child murder. As a study into the methods and motivations of a serial killer *M* is peerless, the ethical dilemmas posed in the final reel are as intelligent and disturbing as any subsequent thriller. Just hearing someone whistle *In the Hall of the Mountain King* (Hans' pre-murder ritual) sends a chill down the spine. This was Lang's first sound film but also one of his last German productions. Like many in the film industry he fled the country.

The influence of these early films lay not only in their visual impact on audiences worldwide but also in the migration of German talent in the 1930s following the ascension of Hitler's National Socialist party. It would be difficult to imagine Dracula's gothic castle without referring to these expressionist films but far harder to see *The Black Cat* (1934, US) being the product of anyone other than a member of the German *avant garde* cinema movement. This left the German film industry in disarray. Censorship and classification systems for film were introduced which saw *M* banned. Film companies turned to comedies and eventually the state took over the main studios to produce entertainment as well as propaganda. Rebuilding a credible world cinema would prove to be a long task.

A popular stream of films emerged in the early 1960s that, although based upon the crime genre, were lurid enough to be classed as horror films. Their inspiration came from the work of the prolific British writer Edgar Wallace and can in many ways be seen as a German precursor to the Italian giallo film. Like the giallo they were populated with stars from abroad in order to market them internationally and often cut and dubbed to match the appropriate territory. The main producers of krimi (crime films) were Rialto Film who began with *Der Frosch Mit Der Maske* (1959) and continued until the series' cancellation in the early 1970s, by which time they had become so similar to giallo they were being co-produced with Italy and even directed by Italians. These included the sleazy girls' school killer film *What Have You Done To Solange?* (1971) and Rialto's final krimi *Edgar Wallace – Das Rätsel des silbernen Halbmonds* (*Seven Blood-Stained Orchids*, 1971), directed by Umberto Lenzi. The combination of macabre and often bizarre murders, the presence of human skulls and the sounds of gunshots are the series' leitmotifs, and were extremely popular, with Rialto producing as many as four films a year. Other companies also produced their own Wallace films using a similar template, the most notable being *Circus of Fear* (1966), a whodunnit featuring Christopher Lee as a lion tamer scarred in the line of duty and krimi regular (and future rent-a-nutter) Klaus Kinski. But the real star is the deranged and twisted plot which makes full use of the circus environment to create a bizarre atmosphere, a sort of *Santa Sangre*-lite, as a jealous knife-thrower is placed under suspicion when an errant blade ends up protruding from his assistant's throat in front of a live audience.

Far removed from the krimi in terms of style, though not subject matter, is Ulli Lommel's *Die Zärtlichkeit der Wölfe* (*Tenderness of Wolves,* 1973), a chilling examination of the murders of Fritz Haarmann.

Lommel, a long-term member of Rainer Werner Fassbinder's entourage, continued his career both in front of and behind the camera – he often wrote, directed, produced and even starred in his films – in both high art (Fassbinder's *Effi Briest* [1974]) and in the horror/exploitation genres. Although drawn to occasionally controversial historical works (he stars as Goebbels in his *Adolf und Marlene* [1977]) and comedy, he always seems to return to the horror film, most notably his Boogeyman films, slashers featuring a killer who is enraged by mirrors and kills in a vaguely supernatural way, often making good use of household implements and gardening tools. After the enjoyable reincarnated witch shocker *The Devonsville Terror* (1983), his films began to show their increasingly minuscule budgets. Lommel's determination to continue was admirable, despite the poor reception of *Bloodsuckers* (1998), an interesting concept about a girl who wants to become a vampire, revealing the good and bad in vampire societies, and *Zombie Nation* (2004). In *Cannibal* (2006), Lommel partly returned to the claustrophobic realm that had shown him to be such a talent in *Die Zärtlichkeit der Wölfe*, telling another 'true' tale of cannibalism, this time controversially close to the case of Armin Meiwes, who admitted eating his lover Bernd-Jürgen Brandes, but insisted that the act was consensual.

Die Zärtlichkeit der Wölfe uncomfortably blended art with horror but remains at least partially discreet in its depiction of atrocity, unlike that of Germany's most controversial director, Jörg Buttgereit. Buttgereit had been making shorts and super 8mm epics for some time and at the age of just 24 achieved international notoriety for his art-shocker *Nekromantik* (1987). Robert and Betty have an unhealthy attraction to death, which is fortunate as Robert works cleaning up crime scenes and has managed to obtain a full, if somewhat decomposed, corpse for the pair to enjoy sexual games with. Buttgereit takes this highly taboo subject matter and refuses to spare the audience any of the couple's sordid games, a gruelling experience not helped by the low-grade film-stock, which somehow makes the events seem even more depraved. Countering this is his use of cinematic devices – flashbacks and the reverse skinning of a rabbit – to emphasise the nature of life, death and the viewer's relationship to what they are watching. His follow-up, *Der Todesking* (1990), is more overtly artful, almost Peter Greenaway in its structure, as seven tales of suicide and pain, one for each day of the week, are told through the passing of time mirrored in the increasing decomposition of a corpse floating down a river. Though not as sensational as *Nekromantik*, save a scene in a deliberate nod to video nasties where a man has his penis chopped off with shears in a Nazi torture chamber, the film's tone is so unrelentingly depressing as to make it devoid of exploitation. Returning to the world of *Nekromantik* in 1991, the story continues as a young nurse develops an unhealthy obsession with the body of *Nekromantik*'s dead hero, trying desperately to hide the evidence of her necrophilic sexual dalliances from her new boyfriend. The effect of a larger budget results in a more brazenly portrayed series of depravities and less murky cinematography but the longer running time and the more elaborate structural elements make this a less unnerving experience, but only just. Not so in *Schramm* (1993), to date Buttgereit's last feature, a blend of the ultra-hardcore gore and necrophilia of the *Nekromantik* films with the bleak pessimism of *Der Todesking*. A fractured flashback from the mind of dying serial killer Lothar Schramm, the shy working man who hides his loneliness by getting sexual gratification drugging, abusing, killing and keeping girls, the tone is sombre and deeply unpleasant, especially when a particularly popular 'girlfriend' of his begins to become overbloated in her decomposition. Schramm's self-loathing leads him to nail his penis to his coffee table to alleviate his guilt, but to no avail. It's taut, nihilistic and virtually unwatchable due to the quality of the filmmaking and its unflinching but artistic outlook.

Recently, the German horror film has moved in two major directions. There's the fantastical horror, normally filmed for the international market, as seen in *Legion of the Dead* (2001). Uwe Boll is a one-man powerhouse of prime-concept, gory but inept horror video game franchises such as *House of the Dead* (2003), which manages to waste Jürgen Prochnow,

Alone in the Dark (2005), which manages to waste Christian Slater, and *BloodRayne* (2005), which manages to waste everyone. Secondly, there is the return to the krimi film as seen in *Anatomie* (2000), in which Franka Potente's medical student uncovers a sinister conspiracy when a man she has met on a train suspiciously ends up on her dissecting table, and *Antikörper* (*Antibodies,* 2005), a disturbing and occasionally graphic film set around the interrogation of a notorious sex killer. Like *The Silence of the Lambs* (1991) the film involves the mind games played by killer Gabriel Engel. The murderer they have in custody is known to be responsible for the deaths of over a dozen boys, and possibly connected to the rape and murder of a 13-year-old girl. But is Engels responsible or is there another killer on the loose?

The influence of German literature and horror filmmaking – would there have been *Edward Scissorhands* without *Der Struwwelpeter*, or Dorian Gray without Faust? – continues to this day primarily because of its striking use of aesthetics, its fascination with the macabre and fantastical as well as its relationship of shape and form to fractured psychoses.

Spanish Horror Cinema

The history of Spain in the twentieth century has had a direct impact on the way that it has produced films. Although film production was prevalent there weren't the early international successes that other European markets enjoyed and the only 'horror' film (for it is both graphic and psycho-sexually disturbed), *Un Chien Andalou* (1928), was aimed more at the art market. Its co-director Luis Buñuel was exiled a few years later. Following the Franco uprising in 1936, the state imposed censorship in almost all parts of life. Various measures were instigated to control film production either through quotas, promoting nationalist cinema, or minimum budget levels, to prevent cheap productions that were being made because of the quotas. As a result many films sought co-financing outside Spain and, in the case of more contentious material, different versions were produced to suit different, often more liberal, markets – a practice that the Franco regime would also try to curtail. In this environment the process of creating an indigenous horror industry would appear to be difficult. But, slowly, one did emerge.

The super-prolific Jesus Franco started his series of Dr Orloff films, a kind of mad medical doctor pulp with the artistic intention of *Les Yeux sans visage* (which he would end up remaking in 1988 as *Faceless*), with his 1962 *Gritos en la noche* (*The Awful Dr Orloff*). The film played upon themes of death, longing, torture and sex that would be the thematic backbone of his numerous future productions. Although it fell foul of the local censors the scenes of sadism and nudity were not as heavily trimmed as might be expected. Franco continued his assaults on the film world via every conceivable genre but mainly returning to marketable exploitation themes, including family-friendly torture in a series of Fu Manchu films in 1968. An overview of his career could easily fill this book. Countless vampire films, Frankenstein films and Orloff films vie alongside non-genre women-in-prison films and de Sade adaptations, often with a burlesque show somewhere in the running time and often with a jazz soundtrack. At his best – *Vampiros Lesbos* (1970), *Necronomicon* (1967), *Jack the Ripper* (1977) – Franco can produce a stylish blend of art, horror and eroticism. At his worst – *Erotikill* (1973), *El Conde Dracula* (1971) and too many more to mention – his films can be messy and juvenile. Franco generally sought funding further afield and, although popular, didn't have more than a passing influence on home turf.

The film that finally did launch Spanish horror was *La Marca del Hombre-lobo* (*Frankenstein's Bloody Terror*, 1968), written by and starring long-time Universal Horror aficionado Jacinto Molina as the cursed wolfman Waldemar Daninsky. Molina was forced to come up with a screen name, Paul Naschy, to give the film international appeal. The combination of brash violence and werewolf-on-vampire action (making its US title seem decidedly inappropriate), not to mention the widescreen 3-D visuals in crisp 70mm, ensured the film's success, heralding a new age of fantasy horror that was often laced with sexuality and nudity. The film's fantastical nature meant it passed through the state censor's hands with only minor alterations, most notably that the werewolf could not be from Spain because this might harm nationalistic feelings. The model proved both irresistible and profitable, and Naschy would go on to star as a number of Universal-style monsters including a mummy, Dracula and a turn as a Quasimodo-style hunchback in the macabre *El Jorobado de la Morgue* (*Hunchback of the Morgue,* 1972). But he always returned to Waldemar Daninsky. In 1972, Naschy wrote and starred in over half a dozen horror titles, each eagerly lapped up by an audience revelling in the twin delights of the forbidden and the entertaining. Although he had started a trend there was no way he was going to maintain a monopoly on the market and other filmmakers used this opportunity to put their own fantastical visions on the big screen.

Amando de Ossorio became renowned for a series of films featuring the Blind Dead. Often referred to as Knights Templars, these horrific creations are seen terrorising the Spanish countryside hundreds of years after their presumed execution. In each of the films their eyes have been removed, either pecked out by birds or burned by torches. The set pieces generally revolve around the torture and execution of nubile girls but it's the Blind Dead themselves that are so strikingly memorable across the four-film series, beginning with *La Noche del terror ciego* (1971) and ending with *La Noche de las gaviotas* (1975). They gallop on spectral steeds in eerie slow motion, their decayed capes flapping in the night wind, dead dust mingling in the fog as their sightless eyes seek another victim. The Blind Dead have been viewed as a metaphor for Franco's iron-like grip on Spain through fear and religion. Regardless of intention the atmosphere created is one of surrealistic and unstoppable dread and of helplessness in the face of supernatural tyranny.

Argentinean-born León Klimovsky, who formed a brief and fruitful collaboration with Naschy, proved that his old-school filmmaking techniques were perfect for creating atmospheric in-camera effects on relatively modest budgets and tight shooting schedules. *La Orgía nocturna de los vampiros* (1973) and *La Saga de los Drácula* (1972) mark two excursions into vampire territory in between the Naschy films. Like many, Klimovsky took to whatever genre was currently in vogue but his horror output remains amongst his best. Similarly, Catalonian Jorge Grau had been a mainstay director for many years before he made a series of horror films in the 1970s, notably *Ceremonia sangrienta* (1973) and *Pena de muerte* (1973). He made his mark with the shockingly gory (for the time) English-language film *Non si deve profanare il sonno dei morti* (*The Living Dead at Manchester Morgue,* 1974), a film that remained heavily censored in the UK for over a quarter of a century.

General Franco died in 1975 but democracy wasn't fully restored to Spain until 1978. At this point it would be tempting to think that the new freedoms afforded the country would increase the production of potentially contentious material such as the horror film, but actually the genre was entering a long period of decline and almost fizzled out entirely in the mid-1980s. A few figures hung on, notably Paul Naschy (although his output diminished considerably, reduced to one film every two or three years) and José Ramón Larraz, the man behind, amongst others, the surprisingly effective 'lesbian vampires in Britain' quickie *Vampyres* (1974). Larraz's blend of sex, horror and more sex produced *Los Ritos sexuales del diablo* (*Black Candles,* 1982), a controversial but wholly clichéd film about initiation into the black arts with a political subtext that wasn't really necessary. The availability of home video was also taking its toll on the film industry. It would be over a decade before anything else of genre significance appeared.

Arthouse darling Pedro Almodóvar produced the relatively high-budget *Acción mutante* (1993) by enfant terrible Álex de la Iglesia – a deliriously unsound science fiction film in which an underground group of freaks and rejects kidnap and mutilate the rich and beautiful. He followed this with *El Día de la bestia* (1995). His adaptation of Barry Gifford's *Perdita Durango* (1997) revels in the voodoo horror that David Lynch's adaptation of the prequel *Wild At Heart* was obliged by the censors only to hint at. It nevertheless fell foul of the UK censors on its initial release. Álex de la Iglesia uses his visual style and set design to create slick, often gloriously sick, productions that entertain while simultaneously taking in the more human aspects of his plots. More restrained, though often no less visually inventive or disturbing, is Alejandro Amenábar, who uses low-key, often intimate, camerawork to draw his audiences into a world of claustrophobia or disorientation. *Tesis* (1996) is a restrained but disturbing combination of *Hardcore* (Paul Schrader, 1979) and *The Evil Dead Trap* (1988), in which a man researching the effects of violence comes across an apparent snuff film. Amenábar lets his film get right under the skin of the viewer as the investigation gets deeper and more disturbing. If *Abre los ojos* (1997) is more renowned for its remake as *Vanilla Sky* (2001), more is the pity, as Crowe's passable maudlin shocker pales compared with its low-key existential Spanish counterpart. More overtly genre is the English-language film *The Others* (2001), a deeply creepy slow-burner of a period drama set in the Channel Islands and starring Nicole Kidman as the mother of two children who are unable to survive in the open light. The film's use of gothic imagery is wonderfully evocative as events unfold to their emotionally terrifying conclusion. Like *Abre los ojos*, Amenábar isn't so much concerned with his punch line (a trait that seems to have dogged M Night Shyamalan) as the process of arrival – the atmosphere and the intrigue more than make up for any revelation.

The Cabinet of Dr Caligari (1919), Germany

Directed by: Robert Weine
Starring: Werner Krauss, Conrad Veidt

A defining moment in cinema's expression as an art form, *Dr Caligari*'s shocking, deliberately theatrical sets and the melodramatic acting resulted in the film being ridiculed on release as fantastical and unrealistic. *Caligari* rejects any concept of cinematic realism in favour of a warped and fragmented version of psychological or dream reality – the world seen through the eyes of a madman telling a tale of unimaginable horrors. At Holstenwall fair, the insidious Dr Caligari introduces somnambulist Cesare to the curious public. By night Cesare does Caligari's bidding, murdering or hypnotising townsfolk for his own nefarious purposes.

The expressionist backdrops and imaginative set design make the entire experience disjointed and unnerving; the mountainside is packed with curvy triangular houses, Caligari's caravan is monstrously buckled and the undulating cobbled streets serpentine and treacherous, the architecture of a diseased mind populated by extravagant figures of malevolence. The fair is domineering and claustrophobic, its merry-go-round at a skewed angle, spinning impossibly fast. That these remarkable scenes are bookended by apparently normal moments in a lunatic asylum gives credence to their illusory nature, but this fantasy world invades the asylum itself – the inmates are apparently connected by strings like human marionettes, overseen by their own Caligari. It is as though this world is no more real than the tale we have been told.

The film's influence is immense, from the subsequent German expressionist movement that defined Europe's finest silent horrors, to Universal's use of set design and even Tim Burton's gothic fables. Its combination of art and pulp psychology makes it resonate to this day, residing in the corners of the mind and nagging the subconscious.

Haxan: A History of Witchcraft Through the Ages (1921), Denmark

Directed by: Benjamin Christensen

As its title suggests, Christensen's film portrays the history and development of witchcraft, images of the devil and the persecution of satanists through the ages, sparing none of the details and remaining refreshingly frank. To illustrate the world as seen in the middle ages, the film branches out into an animated illustration of the heavens before

Sacrificial offerings at the black mass in Benjamin Christensen's remarkable *Haxan: The History of Witchcraft*. © BijouFlix Releasing

plunging into an awe-inspiring mechanical realisation of a Boschian Hell with endless bodies being devoured by demons and queues of people shuffling towards eternal torment. And if that were not enough, the screen is set alight with dramatic reconstructions. The Devil is seen in his many guises from towering obese horned priest, to sprightly Pan-clone and scaly beast, with a constantly twitching forked tongue. These are remarkable creations of make-up and acting – *Malleus Maleficarum* brought to life. Nor is the Devil portrayed as slightly evil or a bit of a scallywag. The debasement of the early texts is shown in full – a line of witches joyfully kiss his anus, a convent is corrupted and monks tempted to engage in sex. The Sabbath sequence is as stunning as it is controversial. Following the witches from their homes, the sky becomes filled with broom-riding hags, capes fluttering as they descend on an unhallowed graveyard where they frolic with dancing demons. The rapturous and unholy event is overseen by Satan himself, who gleefully squeezes the life-blood from an unchristened baby and then tosses it into a bubbling cauldron.

Despite its age, *Haxan* remains an affecting, fascinating, insightful work that merges fact and the fantastical to create a unique visual experience.

Dead of Night (1945), UK

Directed by: Alberto Cavalcanti, Charles Crichton, Basil Dearden, Robert Hammer

Walter Craig meets a group of people who he recognises because they have appeared in his recurring nightmare. They relay increasingly strange supernatural tales to him, and it becomes clear that Walter's nightly visions are coming true. So how do they stop the inevitable spiral into murder and madness that Walter's dreams predict?

The horror anthology film is a staple of the genre. It allows the opportunity to take several good tales that don't outlive their welcome, the cinematic equivalent of ghostly short stories, and conclude the film with a twist. *Dead of Night* tells five tales, based on works by, among others, Angus MacPhail (who co-wrote the screenplay) and HG Wells. They're of varying length, accommodating the screen time for as long as necessary. There's the racing driver who avoids being killed in a bus crash following a premonition featuring the vehicle's conductor as an undertaker, Sally's 'subconscious thingamajig', where she comforts a murdered child, and the tale of two golfers who play a round for the hand of a girl, only to have the loser (the other cheated) commit suicide and return as an irritated ghost. The story of Peter seeing conflicting reflections in a cursed mirror is both creepy and surreal as he slowly loses his mind and adopts the persona of the mirror's original owner. The final tale stars Michael Redgrave as a ventriloquist whose dummy seems to take over his personality with murderous intentions (which was also the basis for Richard Attenborough's feature-length *Magic* [1978]). Blessed with imaginative lighting and a superbly executed drop-dead ending – all Dutch tilts and surreal claustrophobic juxtapositions – *Dead of Night* remains a fascinating experiment from Ealing Studios, one they would sadly not repeat.

The Quatermass Xperiment (1955), UK

Directed by: Val Guest
Starring: Brian Donlevy

'I launched 'em and I brought 'em back,' announces Professor Quatermass, failing to mention that his rocket came back to the wrong place, ignited half the countryside and has turned two of his three astronauts into jellybabies. Worse, the survivor Victor is rapidly turning into a life-draining alien...

Nigel Kneale's television series had gripped a nation and provided Hammer with an ideal vehicle for a cinema outing. The extended budget allowed Guest the luxury of some impressive effects and backdrops – the crashed rocket is a powerful image of failed science while the final sequences in Westminster Abbey are convincingly realised. Even better is the make-up work, which renders Victor's skin almost translucent as he undergoes a strange metamorphosis, and the bodies of his unfortunate victims are hideously disfigured, drained of all life. Guest playfully keeps the camera on the move, constantly tracking onto objects or people to enhance the sense of urgency, and is not afraid to rely on audience genre knowledge to increase tension. Victor meeting a little girl mirrors *Frankenstein* (another unwitting monster created by science gone wrong) so that we assume that the child is going to die. But Guest fools us and shows that there is a spark of humanity left in Victor, making his subsequent appearance as 'all vegetable' sympathetic and tragic rather than just horrific.

The Quatermass Xperiment does suffer from two major flaws: the cut down script considerably reduces the more philosophical arguments of the original and then there is Prof Quatermass himself, less a thoughtful figure of science and more a thuggish megalomaniac (actor Donlevy was enlisted to sell the film in the US). Still, there is enough of Kneale's original to make the film a classic and Guest's direction makes the whole affair eminently watchable. Two further Hammer Quatermass adaptations, *Quatermass II* (1957) and *Quatermass and the Pit* (1967), extended the franchise.

The Horror of Dracula (1958), UK

Directed by: Terence Fisher
Starring: Peter Cushing, Christopher Lee

Vampire hunter Jonathan Harker has taken up a position at Dracula's castle in order to stake the evil one. He fails, is turned into a vampire and his colleague Dr Van Helsing has to put him to rest. In the meantime Dracula has escaped. Van Helsing travels to Britain to tell Jonathan's fiancée Lucy about the sad fate of her beloved. But Lucy is gravely ill and the sound of bat wings echo in the night.

Although the plot deviates far from Bram Stoker's novel, this is never-theless Hammer horror at its finest, with career-defining roles for Lee's imposing Dracula and Cushing's no-nonsense Van Helsing. The film pushes the horrific and erotic elements as far as possible within the restraints allowed by 1950s Britian. Lucy in her sickbed is the very picture of virtue until everyone has left the room, after which she removes her crucifix and wantonly awaits Dracula's kiss. When he arrives and bends over for the bite, he draws his cape across her – everything is implied and all the more sensual for it. When she turns nosferatu she becomes truly seductive, and only a staking will stop her lust for blood.

Fisher makes full use of Jimmy Sangster's scripting which contains comic scenes that provide relief from the considerable tension. This, in turn, gives Fisher the opportunity to vary the pace of the film as languid scenes counterpoint the exciting action sequences. When Van Helsing finally locates Dracula, their confrontation is marvellous. The duel between Cushing and Lee is full of energy and Dracula's demise remains amongst the best effects that Hammer produced – his corpse crumbling to dust. He wasn't to remain dead for long. The film was so popular that, like *Frankenstein*, it spawned a long series of sequels and spin-offs.

The Mummy (1959), UK

Directed by: Terence Fisher
Starring: Peter Cushing, Christopher Lee

Following the success of their *Dracula* and *Frankenstein* films world-wide, Hammer made a deal to revive Universal's ailing horror franchises. The first of these was *The Mummy*, based in part on the eerie 1932 film by Karl Freund. The plot is blindingly simple – those who desecrate the Egyptian dead, end up dead. This is based, in part, upon alleged curses that followed the genuine excavations at the height of Egypt-mania in the early part of the last century. *The Mummy*, however, takes place in Victorian England so that the film falls in line with the House of Hammer style. Three years after the excavation/desecration of a tomb has left his father a madman, Dr Banning finds his life is in danger as the members of that fated expedition are murdered one by one. The culprit is Kharis, out for vengeance on those who defiled his mistress's tomb, semi-commanded by the scroll of life in the hands of a modern-day worshipper. Fortunately, though, Banning's wife bears an uncanny resemblance to the long-deceased queen and has some small control over the lumbering, bandaged, dead creature. Fisher uses the scant plot to stage some deliberately garish set pieces. Kharis rises from the swamp slowly, his dead eyes rigidly stare as the mud slides from his musty bandages. When confronting Banning in his home, he takes multiple shotgun blasts to the body, powdered flesh erupting from bullet holes in an astonishing display of squib work. Although the role offers Lee little in the way of dialogue his physical presence is undoubtedly the film's ace card. Hammer's *The Mummy* is a far more graphically restrained film than either the 1932 or 1999 version, but is a prime example of succinct visual filmmaking that is surprisingly even-handed in its discussions about culture, class and religion.

Les Yeux sans visage (*Eyes Without a Face*) (1959), France

Directed by: Georges Franju
Starring: Pierre Brasseur, Alida Valli, Edith Scob

An authority on skin grafting, Professor Génessier rebuilds the face of his daughter Christiane, mutilated in a car crash because of his demonic driving, by kidnapping young girls to use as face donors. Hidden behind an expressionless mask, the world thinks her dead and for the most part, Christiane wishes she were.

Les Yeux sans visage marks the thin boundary between pulp and art. Combining the lurid excesses of the fantastique with a painterly eye for Sadean beauty, the film leaves an indelible mark on anyone who sees it. Despite being nearly 50 years old and filmed in black and white, its capacity to shock has hardly diminished. When the Professor attempts to graft the face of a kidnapped girl onto his daughter the surgery is shown in unflinching and graphic detail as he carefully wields his bloody scalpel. But these procedures fail, and we are shown Christiane's tearful relapse in a series of clinical photographs that chart her deterioration from beautifully reconstructed to irrefutably decomposed. Yet despite its sordid nature, this remains at heart an art film with Cocteau-style dream-like wanderings and beauty in the face of horror. The prevailing image is of Christiane, disfigured to the point that only her eyes remain, wandering in her emotionless mask, a despairing, pitiful figure with no control over her destiny. Denied access to a mirror, she can still see

Tenderness and terror in Georges Franju's *Les Yeux sans Visage*.
Cheongeoram/Photofest © Cheongeoram

herself in windows or, frighteningly, the blade of a knife. From the
opening shot of a woman dumping a naked body in the rain to the final
uncertainty as Christiane stumbles into the beauty of the day, *Les Yeux
sans visage* is a near-faultless combination of high art and popularist
exploitation.

Peeping Tom (1960), UK

Directed by: Michael Powell
Starring: Carl Boehm, Moira Shearer, Anna Massey

Mark Lewis would kill to see a good movie and he does. Stalking buxom prostitutes and 'artists' models' with his portable camera, he films them while he murders them. Confused and shy, he needs a nice girlfriend to take him away from this madness of death and celluloid, which is where his new lodger, Helen, comes in.

Peeping Tom wasn't so much derided on release, it was witch-hunted. No one could understand how Michael Powell, one of the most eccentric but respected of British directors (normally working with Emeric Pressburger), could have produced such a sleazy work. Cut by the censors and mutilated by the critics it virtually ruined his distinguished career. Now it is praised as a classic and often compared with Hitchcock's *Psycho*. Despite some similarities, though, the films are poles apart. *Peeping Tom* derives its psychosis from the father, is shot in glorious saturated colour, is idiosyncratically British and features characters the audience care for. Powell resolutely avoids realism in the quest for a vision of voyeurism that is purely cinematic. In the opening sequence we follow a prostitute to her death from the point of view of the perpetrator, implicating the viewer in the act, but drawing attention to the fact that we are looking through a camera's viewfinder. In that single shot we are both perpetrator and audience, helpless to prevent a crime that has already happened. The most disturbing sequence is reserved for the films that Mark's father took of him as a child, treating the boy as a guinea pig for his experiments in terror. Chillingly, young Mark is played by Powell's son and the father is Powell himself. Powerful, affecting and beautifully shot, *Peeping Tom* is a masterpiece of British cinema.

Sei donne per l'assassino (Blood and Black Lace) (1964), Italy

Directed by: Mario Bava
Starring: Cameron Mitchell, Eva Bartok, Thomas Reiner, Ariana Gorini

Blood and Black Lace proved to be the template for all subsequent entries in the giallo genre and a precursor to the slasher film. Predatory, subjective, roaming cameras, extreme colour lighting, imaginative non-realist composition, sexualised, borderline misogynist, murders and a convoluted plot all combine to make what is essentially a super-sexed-up Agatha Christie thriller. In Countess Christina Como's *haute couture* salon, a black-clad killer strangles fashion model Isobella and drags her body away. When the evidence disappears and more models go missing, the police begin to realise that they have a serial killer on their hands. Of course the police procedurals are secondary to the stylised murder, or rather the stylised stalking, of the victims. When Nicole is abducted by the killer, the screen is awash with changing coloured lighting, bright crimson fashion dummies motionless in the frames, and the stalker dressed all in black, save for a blank, white stocking-covered face. Character movements are highly choreographed, reminiscent of ballet, and everything is stylish – even the killer's tailoring. Bava plays with visual flourishes to emphasise the dual nature of the fashion industry, the glamorous exterior hiding the cocaine, the blackmailing and the infighting, using mirrors to indicate split personalities and the nature of looking. Never a film to let the plot, or even the occasionally wooden acting, interfere with the aesthetics of beauty in the throes of death, *Blood and Black Lace* proved to be too revolutionary for its time. Bava's striking images of wide eyes, focused with fear as the final vestiges of life are drained from the victim, featured throughout his oeuvre – eyes are the window to the soul and reflect the audience's desire to see beauty in death.

As an innovator and a visual stylist *par excellence*, Bava has few equals. His debut, the atmospheric and controversial black and white *La Maschera del demonio* (*Black Sunday*, 1960) established horror icon Barbara Steele as the reincarnation of a witch executed by having a spiked mask hammered to her head. A wide variety of films followed, showcasing an increasing confidence in expressionist colour lighting, including the psychedelic space vampire film *Terrore nello spazio* (*Planet of the Vampires*, 1965) – a clear influence on Ridley Scott's *Alien*. With *Five Dolls for an August Moon* (1970) and *Bay of Blood* (1980), Bava took the template of the giallo film and pushed it further, creating an almost surreal succession of elaborate set-piece death scenes which effectively created the slasher film. *Bay of Blood's* intricate and shocking opening dual death scene heralded the kind of unexpected and surreal murder that would later infiltrate the Hollywood film, usually to gorier but less stylistic effect. At their finest Bava's films are exhilarating and artistic but he is also capable of darker, more baroque horror, as in the strikingly morbid *Lisa and the Devil* (1977). If Bava never quite received appropriate laudation for his work it is probably down to his ability to create trends rather than to follow them.

La Noche de Walpurgis (Werewolf Shadow) (1970), Spain

Directed by: León Klimovsky
Starring: Paul Naschy, Gaby Fuchs, Barbara Capell

Paul Naschy was instrumental in pushing forward the Spanish horror film at a time when the country was still under the Franco regime and subject to strict censorship. Waldemar Daninsky was his signature creation, a werewolf who agonised about his lycanthropy. Daninsky is a character that just refuses to die, even appearing 35 years later on the straight-to-video *Tomb of the Werewolf* (2003), a perennial favourite due to the complexity of the character contrasting with the crowd-pleasing on-screen antics. In *La Noche de Walpurgis*, Daninsky is brought to life by a doubting mortician – 'If I remove these silver bullets then he should come back to life. Aaaaaaaghh!' Daninsky slinks off to a remote village to seek the cross that will free his curse forever, chained on full-moon nights by his insane sister to prevent him mauling the local women. Meanwhile Elvira and Genevieve are trying to complete their thesis on Elizabeth, Hungarian mistress of black magic, by locating her corpse, which, with the help of Daninsky, they inadvertently resurrect. *La Noche de Walpurgis* is packed to the gills with incident and detail, rarely flagging as new subplots pile on. There's gore aplenty as the uncontrollable Daninsky rips through victims innocent or otherwise and the evil Elizabeth glides ethereally to her mesmerised prey. There are the requisite stakings and decapitations, nighttime seductions, Sapphic subtexts, mad women, creepy locals, needless brief nudity and even the appearance of a menacing zombie monk. All this is offset by generally (except for some day for night work) superb camerawork, moody slow motion and deliberately shocking flash editing and jump-cutting. Daninsky cuts a tragic figure – you want him to die because *he* wants to. Crowd-pleasing pulp, artfully directed, makes this a superior werewolves vs vampires stand off.

Les Rouge aux lèvres (Daughters of Darkness) (1970), Belgium

Directed by: Harry Kümel
Starring: Delphine Seyrig, Andrea Rau, Danielle Ouimet, John Karlen

Stefan and Valerie are on honeymoon at the Grand Hotel Des Hermes, a near-deserted opulent art deco oasis, where the only other guests are Countess Elizabeth and her beautiful companion Ilona. The young couple get slowly embroiled in the Countess's hypnotic, loving world of decadence and gentle persuasion but their own relationship deteriorates as a result. Stefan becomes fascinated with a series of murders in the nearby town and begins an affair with Ilona that culminates in shower-drenched death, leaving the Countess in need of a new companion to accompany her on long, sensual, deadly nights.

Despite its 1970s roots, *Daughters of Darkness* is a sumptuous, enticing vampire film and Countess Elizabeth its most beguiling, alluring vampire. Delphine Seyrig gives such a compelling, lover's whisper of a performance you cannot fail to be captivated by her need to be loved, all emphasised by her decadent wardrobe of glittering dresses. If Ilona is more conventionally beautiful her performance is no less remarkable, flicking from wide-eyed terror to the joy of feeding on warm blood. Kümel's film is drenched in resplendent colour, a luscious, lyrical tour de force of aesthetic indulgence. The script is so tight that the ostensibly simple fableistic plot reveals more subtle nuances on each subsequent viewing, always leaving the audience thirsty for more. Despite acknowledging the bloody aspects of vampirism, *Daughters of Darkness* is more concerned with the sensuality and allure of the vampire, the ageless beauty, than the process of maintaining immortality. At times shocking, *Daughters of Darkness* remains one of cinema's most ravishing films with one of its most memorable vampires.

Die Zärtlichkeit der Wölfe (Tenderness of Wolves) (1973), Germany

Directed by: Ulli Lommel
Starring: Kurt Raab, Jeff Roden

'I think he lets them in, but they don't come out again.'

Although separated by over four decades, *Die Zärtlichkeit der Wölfe* can be seen as a low-key companion piece to Fritz Lang's *M*. Lommel's film is steeped in the brown, dank squalor of the depression, where people are forced to do desperate things to survive. In such a climate of disorder and deprivation, a man like Haarmann (based on real-life serial killer Fritz Haarmann) can stay undetected far longer – what is one more boy's corpse in a city of the dead? Kurt Raab (who wrote the script) had been eager to play the role of the paedophile cannibal for some time and his performance here is nothing short of remarkable: cold stares, a thin half-smile and an air of almost innocence. He is open about his homosexuality but his neighbours care more about his ability to provide the meat-deprived locals with pork. Haarmann runs dodgy deals but, coerced into the Midnight Mission by the police, his activities go unconfronted. This leaves him able to stalk his prey with impunity – offering 'suitable' boys shelter from the harsh Hanover streets. In his room he plies them with brandy, strips them and, at the height of his sexual ecstasy, strangles them before drinking the blood that pulses ever weaker from their lily-white necks. The following morning he cradles the naked corpse, gently stroking it, tender and loving. The contrast between the brutality of the crimes and his tenderness towards his victims is difficult to reconcile and makes the film so genuinely chilling.

Die Zärtlichkeit der Wölfe is Lommel's finest moment as a director, matching characterisation with the precision and unflinching horror of the murders, but filmed with economy and restraint.

The Wicker Man (1973), UK

Directed by: Robin Hardy
Starring: Edward Woodward, Christopher Lee

Like many innovative British films of the era (*Performance* [1970], *Don't Look Now* [1973]) *The Wicker Man* was viewed with incredulity by the studios. Over time, though, it has rightly taken its place in the select canon of truly great British films. Key to its success is the manner in which the remote community is viewed by both the audience and the lead character Sergeant Howie. Howie, a devout, borderline fanatical, Christian, takes it on himself to investigate the case of a missing girl on an isolated island, whose community is led by Lord Summerisle. Howie is appalled to find that the island practices (what he considers to be) Paganism, teaching children about the phallic symbolism of the maypole and engaging in nighttime orgies. It dawns on him that the missing girl may not be dead, but has been kidnapped for use as a sacrifice to appease the gods to deliver better crops. *The Wicker Man* is an almost anthropological study of a traditional non-Christian British community but set in a contemporary world that has rejected state religion. For Howie the society is inconceivable and blasphemous, for the audience it is a fascinating insight into half-forgotten ritual – Frazer's *The Golden Bough* with a horrific twist. And what a twist it is, as Sergeant Howie's conceptually and protractedly disturbing fate is made more terrifying by the gleeful dancing of the islanders who, ultimately, mean him no ill feelings but require him for a greater good. With a soundtrack so full of folk songs it's nearly a musical, a cracking script from Anthony Shaffer and uniformly superb acting, *The Wicker Man* is a true oddity: a finely observed, unsettling film whose images linger in the mind long after its conclusion. We don't need to tell you to avoid the 2006 travesty of a remake like the plague.

Suspiria (1977), Italy

Directed by: Dario Argento
Starring: Jessica Harper

Suzy's enrolment at a top dance academy gets off to a bad start as the first pupil she encounters is murdered horribly. Suzy's stay on campus seems doomed to failure. With her health deteriorating, maggots raining from the ceiling and the teachers seeming to leave every night (while their footsteps go in the opposite direction), maybe there's something connected with the academy's past – not just a school for dance but of the occult as well.

The words subtle and realistic are not in *Suspiria*'s vocabulary. From the start, Argento immerses the viewer in a strange, disturbing and vicious world. A girl peers out of the window into the blackness of the night. Malevolent eyes stare back. An arm smashes a window and forces her head through the adjacent pane. Screaming, she tries to escape her attacker to no avail. Repeatedly stabbed, trussed up and dumped through an ornate glass ceiling she plummets to earth only to be jerked into a hanging position before she reaches the floor. Shards of glass and the remnants of the ceiling have pinned a passing student to the ground, her head dissected, her body impaled to the floor like an entomologist's first display attempt. The sustained violence of the opening scene with its astonishing brutality and ear-bursting volume, means that Argento can get on with engaging us in the mystery rather than bombard us with further brutalities... for a while, at least. The powerful use of strong coloured lighting gives the academy a magical feel – we know that the place is evil without the murders. *Suspiria* is about mood, style and execution; narrative coherence and plausible dialogue are secondary.

Frequently accused of misogyny, a matter not helped by his insistence on portraying the gloved killer in most of his work himself, Argento's films are gloriously technical exercises in cinema. His camera restlessly glides from one shot to the next for purely visual reasons, creating an exhilarating cross between Hitchcock and grand opera. Argento's victims are inevitably beautiful and exquisitely dressed even as they are brutally and graphically butchered by their off-screen assailants. Argento's obsession with insects and the writing process are major thematic devices that appear in many of his works. In *Profondo Rosso* (*Deep Red*, 1975) the protagonist is involved in research into the telepathic power of insects but this is just another layer of surrealism in a film whose few but exceptionally graphic murders are contrasted with eerie flashbacks of scratched records, childhood nursery rhymes and axe-murdered parents. *Suspiria*'s semi-sequel *Inferno* relies even less on any idea of narrative cohesion, what plot there is (another search for the books of the Three Mothers) merely a MacGuffin for an extended series of set pieces filmed like a blood-drenched opera. *Tenebrae* (1982) saw a return to giallo roots before he made the strangely delirious severed head and psychic fly schoolgirl killer flick *Phenomena* (1985), a moderate collaboration with George A Romero, *Due occhi diabolici* (*Two Evil Eyes*, 1990) and the highly controversial *Stendhal Syndrome* (1996), in which he cast his daughter Asia as the victim of a brutal rapist killer.

L'aldilà (The Beyond) (1981), Italy

Directed by: Lucio Fulci
Starring: Catriona MacColl, David Warbeck, Cinzia Monreale

The book of Eibon tells the locations of the seven gates of Hell and unfortunately Liz has inherited a Louisiana hotel that's parked slap bang on one of them, a hotel that's suffered its fair share of death and despair including the brutal lynching and crucifixion of a writer some 50 years ago. Before you can say 'Necronomicon', strange accidents and super-natural occurrences are sprouting all around with only Dr John on hand to save the day.

As an exercise in coherence, *The Beyond* is perhaps not the greatest of successes, but in terms of unadulterated gruesomeness, entertain-ment and atmosphere it is up there with the best, a visual essay in horror. Predating *Buffy's* Hellmouth by over a decade, the legions that spew forth from the gate of Hell are unlikely to greet any primetime TV screen in the near future. As soon as Liz has moved into the hotel a worker falls from some scaffolding, the local plumber has his eye gouged out by a water-logged corpse and the spirit of the writer spews blackened blood over the bathroom. To make matters worse, research into the hotel at the local library results in the graphic death of the inves-tigator, his face slowly devoured by tarantulas. Add an army of the undead, surreal landscapes of tortured artists, sepia-toned flailings, mysterious blind harbingers and multiple deaths by eyeball abuse and you have a gleefully grotesque, surreal and exceptionally gory mix of zombies, demonism and bizarre murder. A downbeat ending amidst a barren landscape of Hell is merely the icing on the cake that takes its cues as much from the paintings of Pieter Bruegel the Elder as the Lovecraftian literature that inspires its backstory.

Lucio Fulci represents the epitome of the mainstream Italian horror film director because his career reflects commercial Italian cinema in a bewildering number of genres. However, it is in the field of horror that he clearly found a way of expressing his art. In *Zombie Flesh Eaters* (*Zombi 2,* 1979), marketed as a sequel to *Dawn of the Dead*, Fulci relocates Romero's undead from urban nightmare to an isolated exotic island setting. This allows for some effective and particularly gruesome prosthetic effects work including (the often censored) sequence where a character slowly has her eyeball impaled on a protruding splinter of wood. Further undead appear in *City of the Living Dead* (1980), a surrealistic zombie film founded on Catholic rather than Haitian tradition featuring outrageous bloodletting, including the (again, often censored) protracted sequence where the heroine vomits up her own intestines. Fulci's career became, if anything, more controversial with the release of the ill-advised and misogynist *New York Ripper* (1982), a film whose notoriety is only tempered by the surreal quirk of its rapist/butcher character who feels compelled to quack like a duck as he murders, a bizarre character trait that had roots in Fulci's earlier giallo *Don't Torture a Duckling* (1972). Fulci's strengths as a director lie in his ability to spot trends and respond to them in a way that makes the films his own.

La Morte vivante (The Living Dead Girl) (1982), France

Directed by: Jean Rollin
Starring: Marina Pierro, Françoise Blanchard

Recently deceased Catherine Valmont is revived from her eternal slumber when some toxic waste is irresponsibly dumped near her tomb. When her childhood blood-sister Hélène hears the tune from their old musical box over the telephone, she knows that Catherine is alive. But Catherine has an uncontrollable hunger and has begun to feast upon the living. Hélène returns to the chateau to care for her sister and dispose of the partially devoured bodies.

Jean Rollin's finest film combines the lyrical poetry of his other works with a strong script and exceptional acting. You feel for Catherine and her tragic curse, you sympathise with Hélène. Naked, gorged with blood, Catherine plays a melancholy tune on her piano, but this is no cheap exploitation, it is the moving attempt of an unnatural creature to grasp any humanity within her that remains. Françoise Blanchard's portrayal of the titular character is haunting – a trailing hand on a rocking horse, a desperate glance, tears streaming down her face in remembrance of times past – which makes the exceptionally violent deaths all the more disturbing in their futility. Rollin's effortless mixing of past and present is never confusing and always relevant, his camera slow and restrained. Truly an emotional, sad, beautiful work of rare maturity.

Spoorloos (The Vanishing) (1988), Netherlands

Directed by: George Sluizer
Starring: Gene Bervoerts, Johanna Ter Steege, Bernard-Pierre Donnadieu

One of the most compelling and disturbing thrillers ever made, this film lingers in the mind for days after viewing; it contains virtually nothing in its imagery or language to warrant a high certification but has a psychological effect that is devastating. The premise is so simple: Saskia keeps having dreams about herself and her boyfriend Rex being golden eggs drifting in an empty void. Three years later Rex starts having similar dreams. He has spent this time searching for Saskia after she mysteriously disappeared at a motorway service station. His devotion to finding out what happened to her has cost him dearly, a matter not helped by postcards he receives from Raymond, who claims to know about the vanishing.

What also sets this film apart from the run-of-the-mill thriller is how underplayed it is. The premise is so simple that it is ideally suited to Sluizer's matter-of-fact direction. This economy of style is deceptive as the film plays havoc with chronology and doesn't signpost this fact. After Saskia disappears we are more formally introduced to Raymond but it is some time before it is made clear that these scenes are set prior to Saskia's abduction. Throughout the film there are references to Saskia's dream, although we are unaware until the very end that it is actually a premonition of her fate. The horror lies in an ordinary man, almost too ordinary, concentrating on perpetrating a motiveless crime for the whim of 'the spirit of contradiction'. Subtle, quiet and wholly convincing, *Spoorloos* is one of the most memorably nasty of psychological horror films, and there's not a drop of blood spilled. In an almost inconceivably bad move, Sluizer remade the film in Hollywood five years later, completely diminishing the effect of the original.

Dellamorte Dellamore (Cemetary Man) (1994), Italy

Directed by: Michele Soavi
Starring: Rupert Everett, François Hadji-Lazaro, Anna Falchi

Dellamorte Dellamore is one of the most warped horror films to emerge in many years, a surreal slapstick splatter comedy concerning the profundity of the afterlife and the nature of the soul. Philosophy and religion rub shoulders with lashings of sex and violence to make this the most unlikely of comedies. Based upon a side character in Tiziano Sclavi's famous *Dylan Dog* comics (from which Sclavi's novel derived), this is horror that is at once extreme and profound.

Francesco Dellamorte (Dellamore from his mother's side) is the resident caretaker at the local gothic cemetery who, along with his nearly mute assistant Gnaghi, looks after the deceased. By looking after we do, of course, mean blowing their brains out with custom dum-dum bullets or slicing their skulls in two with a spade should they awaken in the week following their demises. It's a public service that goes unrecognised and unrewarded but, still, it's a job. Whenever he can get to have a relationship with a woman (he only really meets the recently widowed and the geriatric) he still has the stigma of impotency attached to him by the local thugs.

Dellamorte Dellamore's total disregard for taste and its high quotient of casual, gory violence against members of the recently deceased make for hilarious viewing, even as you know you shouldn't be laughing. When a horrific motorcycle crash results in the decapitation of the mayor's daughter and the demise of a coach load of cub scouts and nuns, the scene is set for an escalating series of outlandish set pieces. Gnaghi begins an affair with the head of the mayor's daughter while Francesco has the seemingly endless task of butchering an entire troupe of flesh-hungry undead scouts. No wonder he becomes unhinged and resorts to killing the living as well. *Dellamorte Dellamore* does ask profound questions about organised religion, the afterlife and the way we treat our loved ones when they are gone, it just does so in a way that is uproariously entertaining, visually inventive and blissfully irresponsible.

Dust Devil (1995), UK/South Africa

Directed by: Richard Stanley
Starring: Robert Burke, Chelsea Field

A body is discovered in Namibia bearing signs of ritualistic abuse, the work of a Nagtloper, or Dust Devil, a shapeshifter who 'feeds from the damned and sucks them dry'. Wendy has just ditched her husband and is heading towards the sea to sort out her life when she picks up the hitchhiking Dust Devil, putting herself at the mercy of a power far greater than she can possibly imagine.

Richard Stanley's enjoyable sf horror *Hardware* (1990) proved that he could make effective and impressive films on a pitiful budget and its success gave him the opportunity to film his pet project, *Dust Devil*.

Filming in Namibia was harsh and the film's troubled distribution came very close to complete failure had it not been for the director's determination to self-finance the project in line with his vision. And what a vision it is. The Nagtloper travels to places where magic is still believed, finding itself in the harsh but painfully beautiful desert. Its very existence lies in the cruelty and suddenness of the wind, its purpose is entirely ritualistic and the modern world cannot explain its primitive brutality. Wendy's romantic relationship with the Dust Devil begins when he explains the creation of the land 'home of the great snake father... created by the thrashing of his coils' as the camera performs an astonishing helicopter shot to show the two of them as insignificant dots amidst a sublime landscape. The ghost town setting of the climax plays on the theme of Leone's classic westerns but Stanley imbues the Western mythology with magick symbolism to far more spiritual effect where ritual and timing are everything. While there are many allusions to other horror films *Dust Devil* is one of a kind – unflinching, grim, mythical and intelligent. Shot with a glowing intensity that feels gritty yet otherworldly, the film's infrequent but intense scenes of exacting violence are graphic but wholly integral.

El Día de la bestia (Day of the Beast) (1995), Spain

Directed by: Álex de la Iglesia
Starring: Álex Angulo, Armando De Razza, Santiago Segura

'I haven't sinned... but I will.' Father Angel faces a dilemma after 25 years of studying St John's Apocalypse. The numerology in the text indicates that the anti-Christ will be born on Christmas Eve heralding the beginning of the end of the world and only he knows how to stop it. Sort of. And Christmas Eve is tomorrow. In order to see the Devil and prevent the birth, Angel needs to be Satan's disciple, and that means lots of sinning to make up for lost time.

    A riot of slick filmmaking and improper laughs, *El Día de la bestia* is a sick ecumenical comedy about the birth of the anti-Christ and the nature of faith. Key to the film's success is the contrast between dedicated Father Angel getting to grips with life in the big city and learning how to be satanic. He starts sinning small – nicking money from beggars and pushing mime-artists down subways (is that actually a sin?) but is soon denying absolution, burning crosses on his feet with cigarettes and, worse, seeking out heavy metal music. Teaming up with rotund death metal record shop owner José María they kidnap TV psychic Prof Cavan in order to learn how to raise the Devil, which they do by etching a pentagram in his new penthouse floor. It's all gloriously unsound, especially when the hapless priest is sent on a seemingly impossible mission of obtaining the blood of a virgin. Like his mentor Pedro Almodóvar, who produced the equally deranged *Acción Mutante*, de la Iglesia is at his best when he contrasts the mundane with the absurd, when societies break down or perceived perversities are contrasted with daytime television chat shows and casual gossip. Full of carefully choreographed set pieces and excellent special effects (like the *Devil Rides Out*-style invocation's bipedal goat) this is the antidote to po-faced religious horror such as *Stigmata* (1999) or *The Exorcist* (1973).

Funny Games (1997), Austria

Directed by: Michael Haneke
Starring: Susanne Lothar, Ulrich Mühe, Arno Frisch, Frank Giering

Horror films are generally considered disreputable, aimed at the young and without artistic pretentions, often by those who haven't seen them. In many ways this is what makes *Funny Games* such a subversive film. Not only is it a nasty, unrelenting descent into helplessness and despair, it is also a film that played not at multiplexes but at arthouses – sneaking under the radar and catching a new audience unawares.

Peter and Paul are two apparently genial individuals who work their way into the holiday home of affluent couple Anna and Georg, on vacation with their son and pet dog. But an altercation over some eggs leads to a siege in which the family's lives and sanity become part of Peter and Paul's increasingly sadistic games.

Funny Games is about implication and aftermath, voyeurism, denial and the viewer's relationship to the atrocities portrayed. The signs are there in the casual tennis clothes Peter and Paul wear, finished off with meticulous white gloves – a pristine offspring of *Rope* (1948) and *A Clockwork Orange* (1971). It is a film about cruel games that the unwilling participants cannot hope to win. Early on, Paul unexpectedly winks to the audience, knowing that we are watching, making us complicit. This makes for uncomfortable, protracted viewing – the perpetrators offer no remorse, no reason for their actions. The only direct violence occurs when Anna, having just seen her son's brains splashed all over their television, seizes the chance to shoot one of their assailants with a shotgun, triumphantly blasting him across the room. But Peter and Paul have the upper hand on both the family and the audience – reaching for a remote control they rewind the film, putting the gun out of reach and dashing any hopes of a happy ending. A cruel, nihilistic and brilliantly manipulative cross between senseless brutality and arthouse sensibility.

Dog Soldiers (2002), UK

Directed by: Neil Marshall
Starring: Sean Pertwee, Kevin McKidd, Emma Cleasby

Dog Soldiers marked a return to confident British cinematic horror. A group of soldiers on a training mission in Scotland soon realise they are out of their depth when they chance across special forces leader Captain Ryan whose team has been ripped to shreds by savage beasts. A series of attacks reduces their numbers and the group must find shelter. Fortunately a local girl offers them refuge in a remote farmhouse but is her offer as good as it seems and does she know the football scores?

Dog Soldiers plays all its genre cards well – the initial low-key set up gives way to a horrific discovery and the group's first encounter with the monsters. Crucially this encounter is dealt with using half-seen shadows and whip-pans as they are overwhelmed in a claustrophobic forest. The exact nature of the beast is left in some doubt (a technique Marshall would use to a greater extent in the extraordinarily tense *The Descent*) – is it a pack of animals, a monster or something more phantasmagorical? By having the protagonists as trained soldiers we are invited to think that their salvation can be achieved by applied pragmatism but it also shows that their enemy is stronger than an untrained man could cope with. The company begins to deteriorate, especially when one of their number has been partially eviscerated, his entrails hastily and sloppily scooped back into his stomach cavity only to get tangled on bushes and suffer the enthusiastic attention of a playfully hungry dog who tries to yank them back out again. These scenes of gross black humour make *Dog Soldiers* simultaneously disgusting and hilarious and in all likelihood the only reason the film presumably avoided an 18 certificate. The werewolves are fast, bipedal and deadly, a sort of furry *Predator* with a howling voice. Marshall plays the waiting game so well you may be tempted to think that he has only limited need to show the monsters but instead he reveals them in all their fearsome glory for an extended and exhilarating denouement.

Haute Tension (Switchblade Romance) (2003), France

Directed by: Alexandre Aja
Starring: Cécile De France, Maïwenn, Philippe Nahon

The original title is about as apt as you are likely to get: gruelling, intense filmmaking that never lets go yet feels fresh and, most importantly, scary. The premise begins simply enough – college friends Alex and Marie are having a break in the country with Alex's parents – but the household is lain siege to by a brutal killer who goes about his business mutilating anyone he can find. Alone in the spare bedroom Marie plans her escape while the sounds of power-tools rev up behind her...

What sets *Haute Tension* apart is that the viewer is on their toes from the very outset – the story is narrated from the viewpoint of a scarred survivor promising dark revelations. In true serial killer fashion the psychotic who terrorises the cast has been fitted with memorable garb, a filthy yellow boiler suit and a tatty cap that keeps his eyes from view and makes him automatically imposing. When he butchers Alex's mother, a wide-eyed Marie watches helplessly from within a wardrobe that slowly becomes stippled crimson with blood. The killer leaves and Marie emerges to find the partly dismembered body lying on the carpet, the mother's head almost severed by a razor, but still hanging on to her last moments of life, suddenly blurting out dying pleas to the terrified girl. Not only is this a film about tension, it's also not afraid to show its bloody hands when any of the killings occur. It's not one for weak stomachs or weak minds, as events become increasingly twisted and hysterical. Were this just an exercise in sadism it would be passable but the confident filmmaking, the superb performances and make-up coupled with a driving soundtrack make this a compelling and visceral ride into a Gallic hell. Writer/director Aja was but 25 when he made this, his second feature.

Gvozdi (Nails) (2003), Russia

Directed by: Andrey Iskanov
Starring: Alexander Shevchenko, Irina Nikitina

A shocking and stunning film from Khabarovsk, Andrey Iskanov's debut is a surreal and nightmarish vision of personal hell. Hitman's identity is defined by his job, a state-controlled assassin wheeled out from his Soviet-era tower block to kill on command. But Hitman is having migraines, vivid hallucinations and an identity crisis brought on by years of indoctrination, drugs and through his forced execution of Hitwoman, the only woman to whom he had any emotional attachment. The solution to his problems seems to lie in his toolbox, where six-inch nails hammered into his skull seem temporarily to provide relief from his living nightmare. *Nails* has an elliptic and deliberately disorientating narrative that matches the fevered mind of its protagonist. Everything is implied with the only confirmation of the story coming in the closing, possibly misleading, voiceover. For the most part, the film is dialogue-free, preferring to bombard the senses with an increasing amount of horrific and surreal footage – overly red bloated lips disengage from the mouth of his slaughtered love, mutant officials drag him screaming into a bizarre interrogation chamber, his apartment block becomes an orange blazing hell, juddering uncontrollably while he slips further into delirium, reaching for increasingly powerful tools to rip, saw and gouge his thoughts literally straight from his brain. Andrey Iskanov's virtually one-man show (he writes, directs, shoots, edits, has a small role, does the voiceovers and co-wrote the unnerving score) is underground cutting-edge horror at its DIY best. Although the influence of *Pi* (1998) and Tsukamoto Shinya's *Tetsuo* (1989) are apparent, it's heartening to find more films out there willing to take this grunge attitude and unleash their twisted tales on an unsuspecting market. Never less than arresting, often morbidly compelling in its grotesquery, *Nails'* hour-long assault on your senses makes it as much a film to experience as understand. Iskanov continues producing outré films that push the boundaries of cinema extremes, including *Visions of Suffering* (2006) and *Philosophy of a Knife* (2007).

HORROR IN THE AMERICAS

North American and Canadian Horror Cinema

Until the advent of sound in the cinema, national boundaries made very little difference to the international film industries. With film a predominantly visual medium, it was only necessary to insert different intercards into the film to tap into the market in any country. But the talkies changed all that. A combination of high artistry, good timing and technical innovation meant that the American film, particularly the Hollywood film, would become the *de facto* ruler of the cinema. Hollywood's great success in the silent era and beyond was through its marketing of star power and in this respect the horror film was no exception. Although character actors had made their mark on the horror film before, Hollywood's first genuine genre star was Lon Chaney, 'The Man of a Thousand Faces'. Chaney used a number of elaborate and painful mechanical devices to contort his features into hideous apparitions and applied his own secret recipe make-up. The results were astonishing and brutal. Chaney elicits compassion with his Quasimodo in *The Hunchback of Notre Dame* (1923) when, sporting an obscenely heavy hump, he is savagely whipped in the shadows of the cathedral for his improprieties. He brought similar, though less romantic, sympathies to *The Phantom of the Opera* (1925), where he stretched his face and pinned back his nostrils to give the impression of a living skull. One of the highlights of the film occurs when the Phantom's mask is pulled away to reveal these shocking features. These were not minor productions but lavish spectacles with hundreds of extras and elaborate sets that played on their sense of literary worth.

Chaney was at his best, however, when he teamed up with director Tod Browning. The pair began their partnership in 1919 and made a number of features together, including *London After Midnight* (1927), for which Chaney wired his jaw with two sets of canine teeth, almost dissecting his head in a maniacal vampiric grin, his top hat and cane poking through the dense London fog to striking effect. Chaney's only sound film was a remake of his earlier *The Unholy Three* (1930), completed before his premature death at the age of 47.

Tod Browning had long wanted to make a film version of *Dracula* and Chaney was the director's initial choice for the titular character, but the actor's illness and subsequent death led Browning to Bela Lugosi, a Hungarian actor who had played the role on stage. Universal Pictures considered *Dracula* (1931) a gamble, concerned that the film's horrific nature wouldn't appeal to a mass market, and they were right to be uneasy. Not only was the Depression on, they had invested large amounts of money converting to sound production. Their prestigious back catalogue was now considered redundant; and, as with many companies at the time, much of their silent film was scrapped for its silver content. *Dracula*, however, proved to be a huge success, making a star out of the mesmerising Lugosi. Suddenly, Universal became the home for the horror picture and the studio produced some of the most familiar horror icons to populate the silver screen.

Dracula was quickly followed by *Frankenstein*, directed by the relatively inexperienced director James Whale, who brought a deep, macabre sense of humour to the proceedings but never allowed it to overwhelm the horror. Although Colin Clive makes for a believably obsessed but ultimately decent Frankenstein, the picture's real star is the monster, played by Boris Karloff, who is represented in the film's opening credits simply as '?'. Capitalising on these successes, Universal began shooting sequels, effectively setting up the first horror franchises, as well as creating original films such as the remarkable expressionist torture film *The Black Cat* (1934) and *The Mummy* (1932) which tapped into the Egyptology craze. The hits came fast and furious and other studios were keen for a slice of the action. MGM made *The Mask of Fu Manchu* (1932) and RKO also tapped into the market with *The Most Dangerous Game* (*Hounds of Zaroff*, 1932), featuring horror's first scream queen Fay Wray in an influential and often filmed story of a hunter whose choice of prey is decidedly human. Kidnapped on a remote island the victims of a shipwreck are given a head start before being hounded down for sport, the severed heads of past victories mounted around the villain's castle like trophies. And then there was arguably the finest monster movie ever made, the peerless *King Kong* (1933). The film has everything – obsession, violence, romance, adventure and, of course, dinosaurs. The fact that the ending is so heartbreaking marks it as one of the genre's finest achievements, and suspension of disbelief in the narrative is absolute.

After the success of *Dracula* and *Frankenstein*, both Browning and Whale were given virtual *carte blanche* to pursue whatever project they wanted. In Whale's case this meant the production of the sublime black comedy *Old Dark House* (1932) and the astonishing effects-laden *Invisible Man* (1933), before he succumbed to a grand sequel *Bride of Frankenstein* (1934). For the veteran Browning this meant he could finally make his pet project, *Freaks* (1932), a film that appalled the studios. Despite the glaring fact that the 'freaks' in the film are presented as fully rounded human individuals while the 'normal' people are paper-thin clichés, they deemed it too horrific. Browning's empathy with his subject (he was himself an ex-circus performer) makes accusations of exploitation harder to justify, but there is undoubtedly an air of fascinated exotica about the production. The film was an expensive embarrassment to the studio, and a worrying portent of what would become acceptable to show in a horror film. But they needn't have concerned themselves for a new Puritanism was engulfing Hollywood in the form of the Hays Code, opening horror to greater scrutiny. Ironically, the genre's newfound success as a mainstream entertainment sowed the seeds for its dilution. The rampant, amoral killing machine *King Kong* was one of the first to suffer the censor's shears and was trimmed a little more on each re-release in the 1930s. Although Universal continued to produce its monster features, it never fully recovered from the effect of the Hays Code. By the 1940s, the magic was waning. With the advent of World War Two, and America poised to join in, Universal's horror franchises began to descend into lazy sequels and eventually parody, though sparks of their former glories did remain. *The Wolf-Man* (1941) saw Chaney's son Creighton adopt his father's name – Lon Chaney Jr – and take the titular role, returning to the character several times, most notably in *Frankenstein Meets the Wolf-Man* (1943), where he battles Bela Lugosi's creature in a role Karloff would have scoffed at. The slow, agonising decline in the Universal series was probably epitomised by the adoption of the studio's monster entourage in a series of films starring the popular comedians Bud Abbott and Lou Costello. The goofy duo first 'Meet Frankenstein' in 1947 where they maintained some horror amidst the pratfalls, but the series became ever more desperate as an array of celebrity monster cameos queued up to be debunked by the slapstick misfits.

While Universal was treading water, a low-budget alternative emerged in the shape of RKO. Producer Val Lewton was approached in 1942 by the cash-strapped company to produce a series of thrillers that could act as the lesser feature on a number of double bills. Provided he came in under budget and with a modest running time, he was given free reign to do whatever he wanted. Rather than concentrate on lurid monster tales Lewton returned to the genre's literary, historical and artistic precedents as well as psychoanalytic theory, to create an astonishing series of horror films between 1942 and 1946. *Curse of the Cat People* (1942) launched the series with a story of a woman's repressed sexual desires manifesting themselves in a killer lycanthropic change that could either be genuine or a figment of her imagination. The film's success led to other challenging works. Robert Wise's foetid *The Body Snatcher* (1945) told the story of a Burke and Hare style trade in human corpses for use by anatomy students. The similarities to the actual case led to the film being heavily censored when it was released in Britain. Mark Robson's *Bedlam* (1946) concerned itself with the notorious home for the insane where the aristocracy pay to watch humiliating shows put on by the inmates at the insistence of a ruthless warden played by Boris Karloff. The film was inspired by the paintings of Hogarth in its depictions of society on the fringes of madness.

Eventually success spelt the end of this exciting period – Val Lewton was promoted to A-pictures and intellectually stimulating horror films would once more become an oddity. In many ways the market for adult orientated pictures was in decline anyway. The advent of television as a mass-market commodity meant that families were staying at home. Cinema retaliated by making pictures that offered something television couldn't – bright widescreen Technicolor event pictures. These cost more than a smaller studio making B-pictures could afford. Physically the films couldn't compete with the slew of epics and intellectually they belonged to a now bygone era. The baby boom generation was growing up.

The 1950s offered America a double-edged sword of affluence and terror. In many ways it was the decade that defined the teenager and the nature of teenage rebellion. It also meant that a large portion of cinema would be aimed at the teenage market specifically. Why? Because kids needed to get out of the house to get on with growing up, and they suddenly found themselves with disposable income. The cinema offered the ideal ground for less demanding, more sensationalist films. But there was also the threat of world annihilation on the horizon. Increasing tensions between the USSR and the USA meant that the threat of imminent world destruction was but a hair's breadth from the idyll of the rock 'n' roll lifestyle. This fear coupled with teen culture resulted in a new kind of horror film – one aimed at atomic age children. If the mad scientists of the previous age were either misguided or downright fascist individuals, the new fear came from a more general science – the faceless white coats behind the Manhattan Project. The fear of the

atom bomb and invasion by Communist hordes fed into a state of paranoia that typifies the 1950s horror film. Radiation causes mutation and a
rampage of destruction as giant ants scuttle across the country in the
excellent *Them!* (1954). Meanwhile alien invasion from other planets is
a thinly disguised metaphor for Communist takeover. In *Invasion of the
Body Snatchers* (1956) the implication is that the Communists are 'just
like us on the outside' but invade society and warp it from within. On the
other hand, it could represent the paranoia of the 1950s themselves –
especially in the light of the House Un-American Activities Committee
witch-hunts against Communist sympathisers.

This was the birth of the drive-in generation and the American
teenager market had an insatiable appetite for trashy films. Exploitation
films provided the requisite hotch-potch of dreamy teen idols, frugging
chicks and gung-ho horror. *How to Make a Monster* (1958) and *I Was a
Teenage Werewolf* (1957) are typical examples of knowingly kitsch
exploitation fodder. One company producing such films was American
International Pictures, which maintained a longevity that many major
studios would come to envy. They gave the undiscerning public exactly
what they wanted, but also provided a rich pool of talent for the next
generation of filmmakers. The company's chief proponent was Roger
Corman, who wrote, produced and directed more pictures than he'd
probably care to remember, including *It Conquered the World* (1956),
featuring a giant killer cucumber, and the cheesy *Attack of the Crab
Monsters* (1957). *Little Shop of Horrors* (1960) is unashamedly cheap
but has witty scripting, an enthusiastic cast (including Jack Nicholson as
a masochistic dental patient) and was made in just two days. *Fall of the
House of Usher* (1960) led Corman into the world of low-budget, full
colour, intelligent horror. This marked the beginning of his cycle of films
based on the works of Edgar Allan Poe, including *The Pit and the
Pendulum* (1961), the witty portmanteau *Tales of Terror* (1962) and the
more serious *Tomb of Ligeia* (1964). While all the Poe films are triumphs
of filmmaking over budget, *The Masque of the Red Death* (1964)
remains the cycle's finest hour. Corman's legacy lay not only in his own

films but in the nurturing of future film talent – on a shoestring, of course – including Francis Ford Coppola, Jonathan Demme, Paul Bartel and Martin Scorsese.

Alongside Corman, low-budget director and producer William Castle was also astonishing audiences with his own unique brand of high concept exploitation and outrageous use of gimmicks. Films such as *The Tingler* (1959), where the cinema seats were wired up to produce a mild electric shock, and *The House on Haunted Hill* (1958), which featured an Emergo inflatable skeleton appearing from the screen, are remembered as much for their promotional campaigns as the finished product, lovingly recreated in Joe Dante's *Matinee* (1993).

By the time the Bay of Pigs had shown the world quite how close we could come to mutually assured destruction (as so succinctly presented in the satire *Dr Strangelove or: How I Learned to Stop Worrying and Love the Bomb* [1964]), American film had absorbed the nuclear catastrophe horror as a sub-genre. The horror film, however, returned to a more low-key approach typified by such films as Alfred Hitchcock's *Psycho* (1960) and Robert Wise's *The Haunting* (1963). Polar opposites in many ways, Wise's work was a fantastical story about a haunted house while Hitchcock's shows the brutal reality of a psycho killer. Both typified the directions horror would take – effects-laden pictures or visceral psycho-killer films.

In the 1960s, mainstream Hollywood began to flounder. The major studios had rallied against audience apathy by producing films that were bigger, louder, wider and more colourful. And more expensive. Given that an A-list feature failure could almost bankrupt a studio, this was a risky strategy, and, following a series of flops, this is what began to happen. The problem wasn't necessarily the size of the pictures but rather their content. The emergence of hippy counter-culture required a different kind of film, and the Vietnam War had begun. Every night on television Americans were watching the atrocities unfold, their soldiers coming home either mentally scarred or inside a body bag. Suddenly the cuss-free, sex-free, gore-free world of the Hays Code-approved film just didn't ring true. Who would pay to see a cartoonish bogeyman on the screen with the horrors of napalm, massacres and madness played on the daily news?

Eventually the studios and establishment capitulated to the new generation. The ratings system was substantially altered and subjects that had previously been taboo were suddenly winning Oscars (*Midnight Cowboy* [1969]). With this relaxation in censorship, exploitation films came out of the grindhouses – or at least the grindhouses got a new lick of paint and invited couples inside. Suddenly hardcore was in the news and hardgore in the local cinema. The new generation of horror film-makers took the maverick practices of counter-culture filmmaking to create a new aesthetic – a gritty, almost documentary style that lingered on atrocities rather than cut away. Some independent producers were hardly discerning when it came to taste, talent or imagination. Most renowned is perhaps Herschell Gordon Lewis, a no-budget filmmaker who introduced hardcore gore to unsuspecting and undemanding drive-ins. *Blood Feast* (1963) features such delights as splattered brains, naked bathing models having their legs amputated and, most notoriously, a woman having her tongue wrenched from her mouth. His later films – *Two Thousand Maniacs!* (1964), *The Gruesome Twosome* (1967), *The Wizard Of Gore* (1970) – continued to pile on the atrocities but their garish comic-book glee renders their excesses entertaining rather than upsetting.

The Night of the Living Dead (1969) marked the start of the independent horror movement, presenting graphic scenes of cannibalism but also delivering a stark political message. This wasn't just a horror film, it was a depiction of the rancour and mistrust in society as a whole. If even a young girl can brutally slay her own mother and devour her, then what hope is there? The film's notoriously bleak ending seemed to decree the end of the old society and the emergence of the new. Similarly nihilistic was *The Last House on the Left* (1972), a film still censored in Britain, where a gang of punks rape and butcher two girls. When the girls' parents discover the gang, they torture and kill them as

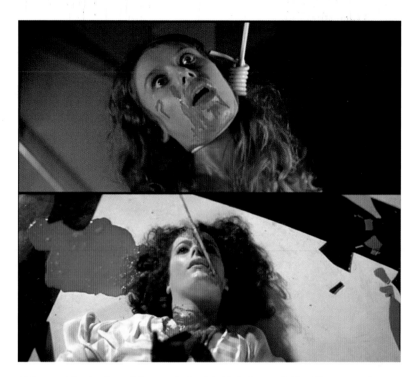

Colour me blood red – stylish operatic death in Dario Argento's *Suspiria*.

Set to kill in *Ringu*.

Who's the smoothest undead of them all? *El Vampiro.* © Casa Negra Entertainment

Sexuality and shadows in Guy Maddin's unique horror ballet *Dracula: Pages From a Virgin's Diary.* Zeitgeist Films/Photofest, ©Zeitgeist Films

A typical example of taste and restraint in Lloyd Kaufman's *Toxic Avenger*. Troma Films/Photofest
© Troma Films

Family matters – *A Tale of Two Sisters*. Cheongeoram/Photofest © Cheongeoram

Unconventional DIY in *Haute Tension.* Lions Gate/Photofest ©Lions Gate Films

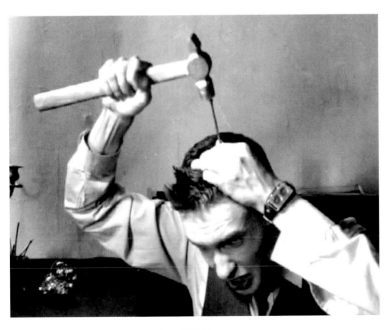

A drastic cure in the hyperkinetic *Gvozdi* (*Nails*).

Don't breathe! Dental treatment the rough way in *Mr Vampire*.

Facing the past – Does my possessed demon look big in this? *Bhoot*

eenage angst in *Ginger Snaps*

Famous horror icons from around the world.

retribution for their crimes. This reworking of Bergman's *The Virgin Spring* (1960) offers an uneasy mix of sleaze and retribution. Made by Sean Cunningham (later *Friday the 13th*) and Wes Craven (*Scream, Nightmare on Elm Street*), it's a familiar tale in the 1970s cinema that revelled in tales of sexual abuse followed by vigilante justice. One of the key selling points of *Last House* was a campaign demanding that the viewer repeat to themselves 'it's only a movie' and the (dubious) indication that it was somehow based upon a true story.

A similar claim was made by the makers of *The Texas Chain Saw Massacre* (1974), the notorious debut feature of Tobe Hooper. Banned in the UK for over 20 years, its power lies in its exemplary use of editing and sound to create the impression of far more violence than is actually shown. This less visibly outré approach to independent horror film-making found its zenith in the hugely successful *Halloween* (1978). John Carpenter's low-budget masterpiece is an exemplary exercise in style and form as well as introducing several horror staples to a wider audience. The combination of scary yet spooky coupled with the newly invented steadicam shots, which gave the audience the monster's viewpoint, was designed for the couples market rather than just the horror aficionado. The film's success did not go unnoticed and a slew of imitators sparked off the stalk 'n' slash boom of the late 1970s and early 1980s.

Halloween was not the first film to depict holiday-based slaying. Canadian shocker *Black Christmas* (1974) had similarly featured the murder of schoolgirls by a largely unseen killer. Although Canada is not renowned for its horror output it has produced a reasonable number of genre films and provided the backdrop for many American films on a budget. Around this time, Canadian director David Cronenberg came to prominence with two horrors: *Shivers* (1975) and the disturbing vampiric armpit shocker *Rabid* (1977), which elicited notoriety for their graphic nature and public funding. Cronenberg later moved into far more personal and psychological body horror territory, making his subsequent films difficult to categorise. Despite occasionally aloof attitudes to the genre, Canada nevertheless continued to produce a steady stream of minor horrors, particularly during the stalk 'n' slash boom, offering such delights as William Shatner in hospital nasty *Visiting Hours* (1982), and Jamie Lee Curtis as the reluctant scream queen in *Prom Night* (1980) and *Terror Train* (1980).

In the meantime, the large Hollywood studios had regrouped and rethought their strategy. Much of the counter-culture generation had joined in with 'the man' and reaped the benefits of larger budgets, provided, of course, that they turned in a respectable profit. Following the success of *Rosemary's Baby* (1968), Roman Polanski's independent classic produced by William Castle, the greenlight was given to shoot a large-budget adaptation of bestselling novel *The Exorcist* (1973). At the helm was William Friedkin, working with William Peter Blatty. The result was one of the most financially successful horror films of all time. Helping the marketing campaign were tales of mysterious deaths, audience hysteria and curses – the whole thing became a circus of notoriety that pushed this shocking but overly worthy film to the top of the box office. As the decade moved on the sombre approach to studio horror began to lighten up, partly in response to the 'feelgood' shark smash *Jaws* (1975). *The Omen* (1976) was enjoyable hokum, and introduced the elaborate, contrived death scene (already a regular in Italy's giallo cinema) to a wider audience where it would eventually reach its logical conclusion in the *Final Destination* films.

The major horror films of the 1970s, both independent and studio, led to the creation of a new set of franchises. Even moderately successful films would spew seemingly endless sequels, a matter exacerbated by the rise of the video player where cover jacket hyperbole gave no indication of the quality inside, be it a known title, or a title-a-like. The slew of slasher films in the early 1980s in the wake of *Halloween* gave rise to a series of increasingly indistinguishable products that came under fire for misogyny and offensive gore. Chief culprit was *Maniac* (1980), a sleazy, grimy, low-budget slasher that featured graphic effects from master make-up artist Tom Savini; indeed this period in film history would see the rise of the make-up artist as a marketable star. A very well-made film with a repulsively compelling central performance from Joe Spinell, *Maniac* is uneasy to watch, especially in the cinema. Although the grime made its way into another Savini make-up film, *Friday the 13th*, there was little chance that *Maniac* would end up fronting a nachos-selling franchise.

With *Jaws* and *Star Wars* (1977), Hollywood had discovered that blockbuster pictures equalled box-office gold. Reaganism (and in the UK Thatcherism) was heralding a new era of neo-conservative capitalism and that meant a new aesthetic – one built on appearances, visible wealth and apparently anti-political footings. The misanthropic liberalism of the 1970s with its political messages and nihilistic prophecies of societal disintegration gave way to the 'loadsamoney' culture. Again the young were the target audience, but no longer were they turning on, tuning in and dropping out, they were watching MTV, listening to pop and partying until graduation – after which they'd become stockbrokers or lawyers. The ratings board pulled back on the 1970s excesses. Suddenly there was no longer a violence and sex free-for-all.

While the initial *Friday the 13th* was passed uncut, subsequent parts of the series were increasingly scrutinised by the MPAA. To compensate, the deaths became more outlandish and less brutal. Wes Craven's *A Nightmare on Elm Street*'s shocking savagery only escaped censorship because its stunning surrealist imagery was clearly not based in the real world. The franchise that followed included a risible sequel, a tolerable third film and then a slide into woeful self-parody and knowing postmodern humour. The once terrifying Freddy had turned from an icon of evil, with his tattered red and green jumper and bladed gloves, to a wisecracking pantomime villain. Similarly the dreamlike surrealism of the opening film gave way to pop-video concept deaths that were designed to make the audience exclaim 'oh, gross!' rather than actually feel gross. It mirrored the overall decline in the American horror film throughout the 1980s and 1990s.

It's ironic that the saviour of horror came from *Nightmare*'s original creator, Wes Craven. Although a truly postmodern horror film had been attempted before – Craven's own variable *New Nightmare* (1994) and John Carpenter's criminally under-rated *In the Mouth of Madness* (1995) – it took *Scream* (1996), with its anorak love of the genre coupled with a hip cast, to revitalise the ailing, some would say atrophying, genre. *Scream* was funny, it told you the genre's rules and then generally stuck to them. More importantly *Scream* was scary, tense and gory. The new, improved, teen horror was back, bolstered by a series of high profile films – *I Know What You Did Last Summer* (1997), *The Faculty* (1998), both by *Scream* writer Kevin Williamson – and the phenomenal television success of the sassy *Buffy the Vampire Slayer*. Suddenly horror was bloody but sexy, vibrant and revitalised. Yet it seemed that horror could not escape its youthful *joie de vivre*, as though the vacuous suck of the superficial 1980s had permanently removed the ability for horror to be more than jump-from-your-seat eye-candy, however witty the script.

The Blair Witch Project (1999) took advantage of horror's revival and made clever use of marketing on the Internet to create a hype that lasted all of five minutes and a passable film. Then later that year came a film that would break all records for the genre, *The Sixth Sense* (1999). Ultimately it is as contrived as any pop-music driven teenfest but it achieves its effect via a return to a more restrained form of filmmaking. It is a subdued, creepy and emotionally driven ghost story with only moderately explicit scenes that catapulted director M Night Shyamalan into the limelight. It marked a brief trend in contemplative horror films, of ghost tales, of more spiritual or traditional scares. It was a trend that seemed worldwide, especially in the wake of Hideo Nakata's *Ringu*, another film that relied on psychological scares as opposed to prosthetic horror. The heady, self-destructive hedonism of the 1980s had given way to a more stable, more caring world, at least in the eyes of the West – no major wars, the fall of Communism and everything had become establishment, even punk rock.

It's not always the case but films often mirror or counter the concerns of society. Horror films had begun to reflect a confident knowingness or a self-assured quietness. However, following 9/11 and the invasion of Iraq that all changed. It would be tempting to see the rise of the new horror film as analogous to that of the post-Vietnam horror film but the situation is more complicated – the general sense of Western angst, the disillusionment of youth and economic uncertainty all add to the social appeal of the new horror. Then there's the free availability of content on the Internet, swapping gross clips on file-sharing platforms – which creates a market for more visceral entertainment. Moreover, the filmmakers that have spearheaded this movement are themselves steeped in genre knowledge that relates specifically to the impressionable films of the 1970s and early 1980s. It is impossible not to see Eli Roth's *Cabin Fever* (2002) as anything other than a homage to this period of filmmaking and *Hostel* (2005) mirroring the nihilism and excess that typified the taste-free era of the 1970s. Similarly, despite their knowingly twisted post-*Se7en* plotting, the *Saw* (2004-6) series of films positively revels in the kind of relentless, humour-free nihilism that merges the plotless anonymity of Internet gross clips, themselves an extension of the Mondo genre, with bleak settings and 1980s style prosthetic work. These are horror films for horror film fans with a widely growing market and expanding group of directors – including Rob Zombie and Darren Lynn Bousman.

It is to this market that studios turned in order to exploit a named back catalogue to a new audience – the 1970s and 1980s period remake. Universal looked to their horror back catalogue to produce Saturday morning serial adventures with gruesome but family-friendly scares with their films *The Mummy* (1999) and *Van Helsing* (2004) and a similar premise was adopted by Disney with its *Pirates of the Caribbean* franchise. The lower-budget sector filled their niche market with remakes of *The Texas Chain Saw Massacre*, *The Hills Have Eyes* and even, unbelievably, *The Toolbox Murders* (2004). The reputation of the originals (or lack of, in the latter case) provided market recognition with the promise of more gore, faster editing and less grimy visuals. The American horror film has come a long way from its inception but perhaps the adage that there is 'nothing new under the sun' is finally beginning to hold true.

The Phantom of the Opera (1925)

Directed by: Rupert Julian
Starring: Lon Chaney

Deep in the catacombs below the Paris Opera lurks Erik, a hideous, vengeful madman. He does have good taste in music, though, and exercises his powers of persuasion to ensure that Christine Daaé gets prima donna status in the opera's production of *Faust*, providing she dedicate her life to her career and ditch her boyfriend. But when she fails to attain the Phantom's exacting demands he decides to bring the house down. Literally.

The combination of grand scale, doomed twisted love, greed for fame and a backdrop of decadent Paris is irresistible, providing the perfect setting for grandiose melodrama with a scale that typifies both opera and Hollywood big-budget filmmaking. The attention to design is second to none; sets of Faustian hells await in the wings, the Phantom's abode ranges from his austere coffin to Christine's impossibly chintz boudoir and the black underground lake with its domineering arches can only be traversed by means of gondola. In one of the film's most celebrated scenes the huge staircase of the opera house's foyer is the setting for the decadent Bal Masque de l'Opera where the Phantom makes his presence felt as a skull-faced figure of death resplendent in a crimson cloak. Despite the Phantom's obvious negative points (he's barking mad and homicidal) he still manages to come across as a figure of some sympathy; he is after all in love, genuinely believing that redemptive passion will dissipate his hatred for mankind. Chaney's make-up is as superb as ever with its stretched nose, sunken eyes and corpse-like pallor.

Although lacking the avant-garde extremities and experimentation of many silent horror films, *The Phantom of the Opera* is a perfect example of a well-crafted big-budget film that can captivate an audience.

Frankenstein (1931)

Directed by: James Whale
Starring: Colin Clive, Boris Karloff, Edward van Sloan

Henry Frankenstein has got it all: a beautiful fiancée, a hereditary title and a place at medical school. Why, then, should he shack up with a sadistic hunchback called Fritz with poor brain-napping skills and a sideline in gratuitous eye rolling? Simple. Henry is raiding the graves and gallows of the land to create a new being. His creation is a success but his paternal skills are somewhat lacking and the confused, vengeful beast escapes to terrorise the community.

Whale's film opens in wonderful showman style with a melodramatic warning that what we are about to witness 'might even horrify you'. Although his film takes liberties with Mary Shelley's novel it stands up well as a story in its own right, the tight framing eking out every morsel of ghoulish dread. Fritz is the archetypal lumbering companion, relentlessly stupid, grovelling and sadistic. When retrieving a brain from the medical college, this hapless hunchback not only smashes the one marked 'Normal', he even swaps it with the one marked 'Abnormal' and neglects to tell the boss. Karloff's performance as The Monster – with groundbreaking make-up by Jack Pierce that is synonymous with the creature's look even today – ranges from wild gesticulations to moments of poignancy. Despite his brutality, we retain a great deal of sympathy for him. In the film's finest scene (sadly censored in many prints), The Monster is shown innocent companionship in the shape of Maria, a little girl. They play with flowers, making them float in the river, but the creature, inspired by the simplistic beauty of the drifting petals, throws the girl to a watery grave.

The sequel, *Bride of Frankenstein*, although stylishly filmed with more accomplished imagery and excellent effects work, falls just short of its forbear by replacing single-focused fableism with unnecessarily explicit moralising.

Freaks (1932)

Directed by: Tod Browning
Starring: Harry Earles, Olga Baclanova, Daisy Earles

Many horror films have poor reputations but few have elicited the condemnation that *Freaks* encountered. What makes Browning's masterpiece so inflammatory is that the 'freaks' are genuine, forcing the viewer to engage with the characters' emotions and lifestyles, even within a wholly fantastical context. It is easier to dismiss them as grotesque sideshow entertainment than contemplate the horror of an active, loving mind being subjected to the casual cruelty of a gawping public. *Freaks* obtains grim closure by showing how these loving people can turn into 'real' monsters, albeit temporarily, when one of their comrades is threatened. Midgets Hans and Frieda are all set to marry but Hans falls for the manipulative, beautiful trapeze artist Cleo. Cleo is after his substantial fortune, formulating a plan with Hercules the strongman whereby she weds Hans and slowly poisons him. But the callous couple don't reckon on the strength of community spirit, for, if you 'offend one then you offend them all'.

The film's message is clear – that the real freaks of the piece are Hercules and Cleo, uncaring, shallow and deformed on the inside, defined entirely by sexual and financial lust. It is the community that is shown to be strong. But even if this narrative hook, the extortion of Hans at the expense of his true love, were removed you would still be left with a fascinating insight into circus life and culture. Browning shows the mundane life behind the glitz: lives, loves, gambling, rehearsing, enjoying a cigarette, preparing new clown gags, even stagehands ogling the girls. Importantly, we never see anyone perform. In some ways we have impinged on their world by being granted this intimate viewpoint. Insightful, moving and compassionate, *Freaks* is a beautiful, if savage, work that has few peers.

King Kong (1933)

Directed by: Merian Cooper & Ernest Schoedsack
Starring: Fay Wray, Robert Armstrong

From exotic tribal rituals to huge battling dinosaurs with multiple violent deaths and a massive primal beast ripping a bloody swathe through a major city, *King Kong* has got the lot. Filmmaker Carl Denham makes sensationalist pictures and takes 'love interest' Anne to Skull Island. However his leading male turns out to be none other than Kong – a giant ape worshipped by the islanders. Denham's motives are even more devious as he prepares to show the 'eighth wonder of the world' to a rapturous New York audience, a plan Kong is none too happy about.

Kong's power has hardly diminished in over 70 years because of one thing – character. Kong never ceases to be a living entity, the purest screen manifestation of the male id. He hates with gusto, he loves and protects with gusto, proving his worth to his 'mate' Anne by wringing the life out of the island dinosaurs with his bare hands. Willis O'Brien's exemplary special effects provided an inspiration to masses of cineastes, including stop-frame guru Ray Harryhausen, and they are still eerily organic. Fay Wray's Anne is not just a scream queen but a gutsy, adventurous lass very capable of standing up for herself, unless she's about to be sacrificed to a lumbering megabeast. By the film's close she has come to respect and even pity her captor, torn from his natural environment to amuse the thoughtless masses. When Kong shrugs off his shackles and stampedes through the city, you cheer for him; when he finally confronts the might of technology, you shed a tear. Magical.

Kong and his offspring appeared in a number of later productions including a memorable tussle with Godzilla, a truly atrocious De Laurentiis-produced remake in 1976 and Peter Jackson's decent mega-budget version in 2005.

The Black Cat (1934)

Directed by: Edgar G Ulmer
Starring: Boris Karloff, Bela Lugosi

Despite the contemporary setting and futurist architecture *The Black Cat* is Universal's most overtly gothic picture in both tone and implication. Newlyweds Joan and Peter are forced to spend the night in the grandiose mansion of Herr Poelzig when the coach they are travelling in crashes. With them is Dr Werdegast, a bitter man who has recently been released after 15 years as a prisoner of war. The war has taken his youth, but Poelzig has taken his wife and daughter. Now he seeks

Bitter rivals Boris Karloff and Bela Lugosi in *The Black Cat*. Universal Pictures/Photofest
© Universal Pictures

answers and vengeance. Poelzig meanwhile is hatching insidious plans to sacrifice Joan in a satanic ceremony, just one of the terrifying secrets hidden in his imposing fortress.

Based upon the stories of Edgar Allan Poe, Ulmer's film is filled with an eerie sense of design and direct parallels to the rise in Nazism that was infecting his home country. Poelzig's mansion is a towering building that mirrors its master's cold, cavernous heart – hiding dark secrets in its bowels. Poelzig displays the bodies of his deceased wives in vertical glass coffins where they remain preserved in all their dead beauty, suspended in their transparent graves. This is the fate of Werdegast's wife, a long-dead but perfectly preserved trophy for her satanic captor. Worse, his daughter is now Poelzig's wife. This is dark, macabre film-making where the real horror is man's ability to control, abuse and debase all that lives. There is no ultimate triumph of good – Werdegast has been driven to the point that he becomes as malicious as the man who has ruined his life, finally getting Poelzig at his mercy and away from the apparently immortal black cat that protects him, gleefully flaying his body in bloody retribution. An allegory for the rise of evil, *The Black Cat* is a morbid masterpiece of necrophilic sexuality, despair and pain. Released just as the Hays Code was being imposed this is a still shocking yet visually resplendent work of disturbing intensity.

Cat People (1942)

Directed by: Jacques Tourneur
Starring: Simone Simon, Kent Smith, Jane Randolph, Tom Conway

Serbian Irena believes that she is descended from a village of witches and that when she is aroused she will turn into a lethal cat-woman. Marriage therefore seems like a pretty bad idea but she ties the knot anyway. However, her desire to be happily married is at odds with her fear of lycanthropic savagery and their relationship remains unconsum-mated. Irena begins sessions with sinister psychiatrist Dr Judd, but meanwhile her hubby Oliver turns to his colleague Alice, whose love for him starts generating the wrong kind of feline attention.

At once fragile and terrifying, Irena represents the raw emotional passion of the exotic European female contrasting with American logical pragmatism – her frigidity is as much down to the difference in cultural outlook as childhood trauma. Her mystique and mood swings make her a fascinating subject, as illustrated by the twinkle in her eye when she plays with a dead bird before feeding it to a panther. Tourneur is a master of light and shadow, evoking the claustrophobia of Irena's world with tight, minimal lighting. The tension is at times unbearable. When Irena stalks Alice on her way home, the superb editing and camerawork keep the audience on the edge of their seats right to the MacGuffin bus conclusion, juxtaposing animal and vehicular sounds for visceral and thematic effect. The horror of the unseen can be a double-edged sword, but when done properly the results are mesmerising and terrifying. *Cat People* succeeds because it provides tragedy and sympathy along with the scenes of intensity. The film was pointlessly remade in a more graphic and incestuous manner by Paul Schrader in 1982.

Tourneur went on to direct further films for Val Lewton, including the thematically similar *The Leopard Man* (1943) and the eerie Jane Eyre adaptation *I Walked with a Zombie* (1943). After many years making exemplary westerns and film noir, Tourneur returned to the horror genre with the moody MR James adaptation *Night of the Demon* (1957) based on *Casting the Runes*.

Them! (1954)

Directed by: Gordon Douglas
Starring: James Whitmore, Edmund Gwenn, Joan Weldon

At the height of cold war paranoia and with the prevailing atmosphere of McCarthyism, few people in America would directly question the nuclear programme or its possible effects. Instead the monster movie, being so fantastical as to be dismissed as pulp entertainment, posed social commentary in the context of mutant creatures ripping up America. *Them!* remains one of the finest examples of the genre and is still an exciting movie. The police are baffled when a remote convenience store and a family's mobile home are discovered torn apart, their owners missing or dead. Father and daughter scientists Dr and Dr Medford are flown in to aid the investigation. It becomes clear that these events have been caused by giant mutant ants, who are migrating from their nest to destroy anything in their path.

As with all great monster movies *Them!* builds up the pace deliberately, before unleashing a grand finale. What sets it apart is its exemplary use of special effects and the eerie mise-en-scène. The film opens with a little girl stumbling across the desert in a catatonic stupor at the horrors she has seen. The ants are fearsome creatures taller than a man,

Menacing insects from the nuclear paranoia classic *Them!*

with jaws that rip their victims apart, whilst emitting high-pitched shrills. These inhuman sounds provide the film with as much terror as the ants themselves. Indeed *Them!* employs a whole arsenal of horror film tactics: sudden jumps, looming shadows on the tunnel walls, suspenseful searches in enclosed spaces, kids in peril, ominous music. The film's open-ended coda, in which the Doctor speculates on the Pandora's box nature of nuclear weapons while the last of the ants is burning, is probably the most succinct and balanced debate on the whole issue. Flesh-eating giant mutants, politics and militarism all in one enjoyably pulp package.

Invasion of the Body Snatchers (1956)

Directed by: Don Siegel
Starring: Dana Wynter, Kevin McCarthy

Miles is having a tough time getting through to people – they're all vegetables. Literally. Cultivated from alien pods, these leggy legumes are replacing the townsfolk while they sleep, assimilating their looks but not their feelings. Miles must try to make the authorities believe his story before the whole country is overrun, but even he needs to sleep eventually...

'At first glance everything looked the same, it wasn't. Something evil had taken over the town.' Don Siegel's paranoid nightmare is a perfect example of lean scripting and tight narrative focus. The film has been seen by some as a vindication of the McCarthy witch-hunts of the 1950s, the perils of allowing your neighbourhood to be overtaken by Communists. On the other hand it can be viewed as the individual standing up to governmental restrictions on its freedoms. Regardless, the paranoia is palpable. The prospect of being 'born into another world... where everyone's the same' may bring comfort and support, but it removes free will and the ability to fail as well as triumph. Siegel tightly composes his images to show the world slowly closing in on Miles, filming the mundane with a slight air of unreality. The bland framing in the early parts of the film make the disorientating Dutch tilt that greets the discovery of the first vegetable pod all the more horrific. The humanoid offspring of these pods are chillingly devoid of identity until they have assimilated their victims. It is the speed with which they replace their human doubles that provides the film with its shocks and increases the paranoia to feverish levels – even loved ones cannot be trusted if they have been out of sight for just a moment.

Remade to reflect contemporary concerns, Philip Kaufman's 1978 version expands the running time and budget of the original to good effect although it remains less focused, while Abel Ferrara's 1993 overhaul places the story in a military and political context.

Psycho (1960)

Directed by: Alfred Hitchcock
Starring: Janet Leigh, Anthony Perkins, Vera Miles, Martin Balsam

Marion Crane is a naughty girl, sneaking a quickie in a hotel room during lunch breaks and scheming with her boyfriend. She has a plan to get away with enough money from her stupid employers to start a new life. Such illegal activities are clearly fatigue-inducing, especially after a long drive, so perhaps she needs a good rest. The ideal place is the Bates Motel, overseen by jittery but amiable owner Norman, who lives with his reclusive mother in the adjacent gothic house.

Years of deep critical analysis and adulation have made *Psycho* a difficult work to view with objectivity. Hitchcock's great trick was to give the audience just one identifiable star, place the action in a mundane environment (although Bates's house is the epitome of the old, dark house) and kill her off before the film is even half way through. He caught contemporary audiences completely off-guard. The infamous shower scene is a triumph of expressionist, Eisensteinian editing, accentuated by Bernard Herrmann's deliriously experimental score. Not a frame is wasted, and if the events following Marion's death seem a little sedate it is because they cannot be topped. *Psycho* ushered in the 1960s with a challenge on acceptability – Hitchcock, the great auteur, even wrong-footed his core audience with a return to grittier black and white stock to make the film appear extra seedy – and provided the precursor for almost every stalk and slash film to come. It's nowhere near as graphic as modern fare in terms of gore or nudity, although Leigh's role was considered risqué at the time, but the film's pivotal scene remains shocking because the impression of savage butchery is so intense. Bizarrely the American censors had more problems with the toilet being prominent in a number of shots rather than the sex and death. *Psycho*'s legacy cannot be underestimated although it is perhaps ironic that this film, the least typical of Hitchcock's oeuvre, is now the film most associated with him.

The Haunting (1963)

Directed by: Robert Wise
Starring: Julie Harris, Claire Bloom, Richard Johnson, Russ Tamblyn

Robert Wise's reputation as a director is sorely undervalued, partly because his résumé covers a diverse range of genres from sci-fi to musical. *The Haunting* shows without doubt that he is master of the psychological horror film. Based on *The Haunting of Hill House* by Shirley Jackson, the film wastes no time in establishing its aim: to scare the audience senseless. Dr Markway has assembled a small group, including psychic seer Theodora and hyper-sensitive Eleanor, to investigate possible supernatural activity at the imposing Hill House. They arrive. Things go terribly wrong. There is no need to establish whether Hill House is haunted or not. Our dilemma, as with the characters, is how long we stay to find out whether the house is genuinely malevolent.

Wise creates a pervasive feeling of unease and dissociation – characters get lost in corridors, angles are skewed and unfamiliar, companions go missing at inappropriate times. The air of helplessness at the house's mighty power becomes palpable. In one scene an increasingly distressed Eleanor seeks the solace of Theodora as the house seems to be persecuting her. The pair huddle in fear as creaks, laughter, thumps and moans surround them in their increasingly claustrophobic room. Eleanor begins to worry that Theodora is clutching her hand too tightly… only to realise she is on the opposite side of the room. 'Whose hand was I holding?' she recoils in terror. As events escalate the house itself becomes alive – crashes at the doors cause them to warp and the increasing use of extreme camera lenses makes the mansion seem like a violent, organic prison. Shocking scenes of brief violence, suicide themes and hints of abuse make for uncomfortable viewing, but the overall oppressive air of foetid malice is what ultimately makes the film so hard to shake on an emotional level. *The Haunting*'s ability to remain the definitive haunted house movie was confirmed decades later when Jan de Bont's technically impressive but wholly anaemic remake laughably failed to be anywhere near as scary, disturbing or effective.

The Masque of the Red Death (1964)

Directed by: Roger Corman
Starring: Vincent Price, Jane Asher, Hazel Court

Prosperous Prince Prospero burns down the local village in order to get pretty Francesca to bed him, imprisoning her father and boyfriend to obtain extra leverage in the nuptial department. Still, he is probably doing them a favour because the excruciatingly painful red death is ravishing the country. With all that grimness abroad Prospero decides to throw a jolly good masque to cheer himself up. But as with any decent bash there are always gatecrashers…

While all Corman's Poe films are triumphs of filmmaking over budget, *The Masque of the Red Death* marks the cycle's finest hour. It is also a perfect realisation of Corman's basic rules of exploitation cinema – give the audience regular hints of nudity and/or violence and put as much on the screen as your budget limitations will allow. *The Masque of the Red Death* is in full colour and looks far more expansive and expensive than it actually is. Cinematographer and future director Nicolas Roeg saturates the screen with eye-popping chromatic intensity. Electric-blue mists reveal crimson-cloaked harbinger monks, brightly lit sunflower-yellow rooms or a white rose engorged with deep red blood. Price's Prospero is unremittingly grandiose in his cruelty, viewing peasants as entertainment and even his guests as disposable playthings. Corman manages to imbue this film with a Grimm air of fairy-tale decrepitude mixed with the Crowleyesque ethos of 'do what thou wilt'. Add a rhythmic sacrificial dream sequence and a rainbow-coloured pretentious ending where angels of death meet up after a tough day at the office, and the result is a classic combination of knowing artiness and *Grand Guignol* exploitative horror.

Two Thousand Maniacs! (1964)

Directed by: Herschell Gordon Lewis
Starring: William Kerwin, Connie Mason, Jeffrey Allen

Although explicit gore in the movies had been around since cinema's inception it took Herschell Gordon Lewis to make it the reason to see a film. Lewis made movies predominantly for southern states drive-ins where low-budget exploitation flourished. When the market for cheaply produced sex comedies began to wane, Lewis had the genius to explore the other chief area of exploitation cinema – violence. His approach was not simply to show violent acts but unflinchingly revel in them. *Two Thousand Maniacs!* concerns six northerners travelling through the southern states who are deliberately detoured to the little town of Pleasant Valley (population 2,000) where jovial Mayor Buckman declares them guests of honour for the community's centennial celebrations. As guests they have free lodging, food and drink, the chance to flirt with the locals and die in hideous fashion. The first victim has first her thumb and then her arm cut off and barbecued. Another is torn into pieces by horses. A third is put in a barrel where huge nails are driven in and then pushed down a hill, the spikes ripping his flesh to shreds. All of this contrasts with the happy yelps and 'yee-haws' of the jubilant redneck town-folk. What sets *Two Thousand Maniacs!* apart is that you are meant to be cheering with the murderers; the outsiders are seen as promiscuous, pretentious and self-centred. Also, strangely, the film has its own diegetic chorus of three country music players who proudly decree that 'the south is gonna rise again' in defiance of their defeat in the American Civil War. In the film's closing moments it is revealed that the town members are ghosts, risen a century after the south's defeat to wreak bloody retribution on the Yankee victors.

Rosemary's Baby (1968)

Directed by: Roman Polanski
Starring: Mia Farrow, John Cassavetes

Rosemary and Guy's approach to procreation starts with a bang once they move into The Bramford, a sumptuous apartment block. Guy's an actor whose luck is coincidentally improving since neighbours Minnie and Roman Castavet made themselves part of the household. But as Rosemary's happy day approaches, she suspects that her baby is going to be appropriated for nefarious necromantic purposes and, with strange chanting, grotesque dreams and dubious herby milkshakes to contend with, who can she trust?

Rosemary's Baby may well be nit-pickingly faithful to Ira Levin's novel but remains resolutely Polanski's film. Even now, the elements that make it so disturbing have not diminished – the fear of violation, psychological delusions and paranoia that your friends may well be your enemies. Polanski's distinct and unsettling use of low, long, static shots followed by intimate but deranged handheld camerawork constantly keeps the viewer on edge. He manages to weave together elements of the surreal and psychological that epitomise his best work. Like in *Repulsion* (1965), we witness the slow psychological decline of the central character and empathise with her by sharing her dreams and hallucinations. Rosemary's dreams invade her 'real' space. Her rape by the devil is shown in a half-drugged state to the loud clicking of their clock as she is ritually marked with symbols by her naked neighbours. It becomes more disturbing when, upon awakening, her husband pretends it was he who molested her – 'It was kinda fun in a necrophile way.' The Castavets are deeply disturbing individuals yet remain believable as 'innocents' because of their age and amiability. The sleight of hand from what we suspect (bad) and what is actually going on (really bad) is classic misdirection, but Rosemary's final acceptance of her role in the proceedings makes the film genuinely chilling.

Night of the Living Dead (1969)

Directed by: George A Romero
Starring: Duane Jones, Judith O'Dea

A small group of desperate people try to survive in a house besieged by the recently animated dead, who are hungry for living flesh. Pittsburgh director George A Romero's debut feature, shot on a shoestring using black and white stock, is one of horror cinema's most defining works. The reasons are many. First is the gore factor – although filmmakers such as Herschell Gordon Lewis had revelled in excess for years, theirs were peripheral films for specifically targeted audiences, almost comical in their garish excesses. *Night of the Living Dead*, however, uses its grunge aesthetic and chiaroscuro lighting to make the gore more affecting and direct; like grainy war photographs of the dead there is a grotesque immediacy and realism. Then there is the taboo of cannibalism, here shown in unflinching detail as hordes of hungry zombies paw over the entrails and flesh of two failed escapees. Also shocking is the way the film plays with audience identification with the characters. The film seems first to focus on Barbara after she has escaped from an attack that has left her brother half eaten and then re-animated, but she basically spends most of the film in a catatonic stupor and our attention focuses on Ben who quickly establishes himself as the 'doer' in a house of frightened individuals trying to stave off a relentless series of attacks. What makes this situation so believable and affecting is that the film is so stridently nihilistic; even a semi-triumphant conclusion is abruptly curtailed in the film's bleak and unsettling coda.

The epitome of counter-culture filmmaking, Romero continued to make politically left-field genre films including the anti-governmental *The Crazies* (1973), the brutal and ambiguous modern day vampire film *Martin* (1977), the garish EC horror tribute *Creepshow* (1982), as well as continuing his 'dead' cycle of films with the anti-consumerist *Dawn of the Dead* (1978), the claustrophobic *Day of the Dead* (1985) and the anti-neocon *Land of the Dead* (2005).

The Exorcist (1973)

Directed by: William Friedkin
Starring: Linda Blair, Max Von Sydow, Ellen Burstyn

Chris MacNeil is an upwardly mobile actress and mother of a nice, normal, rich American teenager with the unfortunate name of Regan. Regan's behaviour starts getting decidedly unbearable until Chris is finally convinced she must seek psychiatric help, but the shrink suggests the behavioural problems might be better suited to a priest as this may be a case of demonic possession.

The Exorcist is the stuff of legends. Reports of curses on set, mysterious accidents and related deaths hyped up expectations prior to the film's release. Audiences flocked to see it. Ostensibly the main source of its power remains the dogmatic belief in evil and the fact that the victim is a normal teenage girl. This last point holds the key to the terror: she is not at fault, the possession is motiveless and arbitrary. The addition of Dick Smith's outstanding make-up work and some truly believable special effects make it all the more unnerving. Whether levitating in her bed (requiring frame by frame painting over of any trace of wires – no CGI help then), invoking telekinetic wrath or spewing a stream of pea-green vomit into the face of the priest, the relentless barrage of shocks are more than a little disquieting. The soundtrack, with half-heard back-tracked animal groans, adds a further frisson, rounded off by generally low-key photography that gives the film an almost documentary quality. It fails in the editing where Friedkin convincingly builds up each scene to feverish heights and then cuts abruptly mid-atrocity, bringing the viewer crashing to earth and diminishing the overall effect. Still, it does retain its power to shock on both a physical and meta-physical level, something that in all honesty can't be claimed of its sequels.

The Texas Chain Saw Massacre (1974)

Directed by: Tobe Hooper
Starring: Marilyn Burns, Gunnar Hansen

A group of bickering teens drive into the heart of Texas and get picked off one by one by a family of drooling cannibals. Terrifying and true...?

The Texas Chain Saw Massacre is one of the most notorious horror films ever, with a fearsome reputation that ensured both its success and consequent banning in the UK for over 20 years. The key to the tension lies in the pacing; once things get going, there is no stopping for breath at any point. It is a relentless and disturbing rollercoaster ride to Hell. The chase scenes are loud and frenzied, the quiet moments so eerily atmospheric you can cut them with a knife, as Sally stumbles through a house whose furniture seems to be made of human skin and bones. This is quite simply totally assured and thoroughly manipulative filmmaking. If examined closely there is very little blood and nothing is depicted graphically; the horror lies in what the audience *believe* they are seeing – in one case, a writhing girl suspended on a meat hook witnessing dismemberment by chainsaw. Hilariously, Hooper thought he might get a PG rating for this!

Despite being completely over the top, with everything done to excess, there is a good degree of characterisation. The main protagonists aren't just cannon fodder but rounded and – shock – even dislikeable figures. But the real stars of the show are the cannibal family, each having their own psychosis, whether it's the gibbering hippie son, the straight-thinking father who owns the petrol station shop with the suspect-looking spit roast, grunting Leatherface or the almost inhumanly old-looking grandpa. If Hooper never entirely lived up to expectations in his later films he only has himself to blame; *The Texas Chain Saw Massacre* is an audacious debut by anyone's standards. He went on to create the EC-inspired *Death Trap* (1977) and *The Funhouse* (1981), as well as the exemplary TV adaptation of Stephen King's *Salem's Lot* (1979) and the larger-budget *Poltergeist* (1982) and *Lifeforce* (1985). He continues working in the genre to this day.

Jaws (1975)

Directed by: Steven Spielberg
Starring: Roy Scheider, Robert Shaw, Richard Dreyfuss, Lorraine Gary

Shark kills people. Must kill shark. It can be difficult, over three decades after its release, to view *Jaws* as a horror film; after all it is the grandfather of the summer PG-rated blockbuster, a commercial cinematic theme-park ride designed to get bums on seats and hands greedily grabbing masses of salty popcorn. But even a cursory glance reveals all the trappings of the genre: the drunken teenage skinny-dip gone wrong, her death-toll signalled by the clanging of a lifebuoy bell; the ominous music contrasted with sudden screams and hold-your-breath silence; a child's severed leg, flaps of gnawed flesh undulating in the currents, slowly drifting to the seabed; a half-eaten body; a decomposing head suddenly rolling out of a half-sunken boat. And yet somehow *Jaws* manages to reign in these excesses through two key techniques. Firstly, it uses the town politics to offset the real monster – the shark is a creature of nature responding to natural instinct but the town actively decides to downplay the deaths in order to keep their tacky tourist souvenir stalls open. Secondly, having set up what is essentially a slasher flick with fins, the film suddenly becomes a bickering buddy film about male bonding. The threat to women and children as shown in the first half is a catalyst for the professional men – a working class professional, a scientist and an 'everyman' – to do their job, which is to restore order. Although apparently criticising authority, *Jaws* maintains a cosy reactionary response to events that is audience friendly and non-confrontational. But Spielberg still kills a kid in this movie – a cinematic taboo that more obviously subversive films shy away from.

Shivers (1976), Canada

Directed by: David Cronenberg
Starring: Paul Hampton, Lynn Lowry, Barbara Steele

Welcome to Starliner Towers, your new, safe home on Starliner Island, a world away from the bustle of Montreal. You can be sure that your neighbours will be people just like you – happy, regular, decent folk all willing to spread an experimental parasitic venereal disease with liberal abandon and invite you into their world of glassy-eyed orgies and sexual experimentation.

Shivers wasn't released into cinemas, it was unleashed. A gleeful orgy of sexual violation and integration, Cronenberg is both relentless and unflinching in his depiction of the parasite's attack. The shocking opening reflects this as the mundane aspects of a couple purchasing an apartment intercuts with Dr Hobbe's savage attack on Annabel. Annabel is wearing a schoolgirl's clothing and the doctor's intentions are anything but clear. It is only later that we find out she was a prostitute and, by then, he has strangled her, sliced her open, poured acid into her stomach cavity and slit his own throat to prevent the parasite spreading. But Annabel had another client, Nick, and before long he's tending his new parasites like pets, encouraging them as they visibly move around his stomach area. Eventually he incubates an impressive brood, all wiggling free from his smoking abdomen in bloody eagerness to find a host, propagating via their aphrodisiac properties. No one is safe, regardless of age (both hobbly old pensioners and schoolchildren are up for a bit of French kissing), sexual persuasion or gender; anyone infected becomes a bisexual nymphomaniac. Although people are savagely attacked initially, Cronenberg seems to be commenting that ultimately they become nicer, happier and more egalitarian when hosting the parasite, making *Shivers* in many ways an uplifting pornographic film for lovers of disease. That the parasites are on the verge of taking over the main city and eventually the world means, paradoxically, that the film has a happy ending with the prospect of peace for all. How sweet.

With the exception of his earlier features such as *Rabid* (1977), Cronenberg rarely makes outright genre films, although strong elements of body horror permeate his most celebrated creations, from the exploding heads of his sci-fi shocker *Scanners* (1981), the mutated grotesques of *Videodrome* (1983) and *The Naked Lunch* (1991), the murderous mutant dwarves of *The Brood* (1979) to the agonising transformations of his most accessible work, *The Fly* (1986). Cronenberg's unflinching and clinical approach to filmmaking has resulted in some of the screen's most intellectual horrors.

Carrie (1976)

Directed by: Brian De Palma
Starring: Sissy Spacek, Piper Laurie, Nancy Allen, John Travolta, William Katt

Carrie White is not a normal teenager. Viciously ridiculed at school for her reaction to her first period, she is locked in a cupboard by her fanatical mum who views menstruation as a sin. Susan tries to make amends by getting her dopey boyfriend to take Carrie to the prom, but Chris and her delinquent beau Billy have a plan to make Carrie the ultimate focus of humiliation by paradoxically rigging the Prom Queen vote in her favour. But no one knows that Carrie has burgeoning telekinetic powers waiting to be unleashed.

   Carrie is a triumph of Brian De Palma's audacious adoption of knowingly cinematic technique. Following the cult camp classic *The Phantom of the Paradise* (1974) and the graphic thriller *Sisters* (1973), *Carrie* employs De Palma's trademark of finely crafted set pieces but, crucially, retains a strong emotional core. If some of the more grandiose scenes from Stephen King's book have been trimmed back, this serves only to focus more on the human aspects of the story. Piper Laurie steals the limelight as Carrie's mother, a towering performance of dislocated guilt and fanaticism, her religiously fuelled abuse of her child punished by crucifixion from telekinetically controlled cutlery. Spacek herself elicits the majority of the audience's considerable sympathy – she may be termed the 'monster' of the piece but her vengeance is as understandably reactionary as it is breathtaking. The final scare is one of the most imitated endings of any horror film, its dreamlike surrealism enhanced by the fact that much of it was shot backwards. It still has the power to jolt no matter how many times you see it. De Palma continued working in a variety of genres, returning to telekinetic horror with *The Fury* (1978) as well as producing the often criticised slasher-esque films *Dressed to Kill* (1980), *Blow Out* (1981) and *Body Double* (1984).

The Omen (1976)

Directed by: Richard Donner
Starring: Gregory Peck, Lee Remick, Patrick Troughton, David Warner

Six-six-six, the number of the beast. Unusually, this number is tattooed on the head of Robert Thorn's newly born son, Damien, a detail he fails to notice because of the boy's impressive head of hair. Twitchy cleric Father Brennan is utterly convinced that Damien is not Thorn's son but the spawn of Satan and tries to warn the Thorns, who simply think he's deranged. But as Damien witnesses an increasing number of deaths Thorn travels back to his son's birthplace to discover some terrifying truths.

What set *The Omen* apart from the run-of-the-mill horror flicks of the period was the number of trend-setting elaborate set-piece deaths. After a slow is-he-isn't-he build-up (he is, incidentally) the film finds its stride with the untimely demise of Father Brennan, impaled by a cathedral spire struck by lightning on a cloudless day. Despite the novelty of the bizarre deaths (most memorably David Warner's stunning multiple angle decapitation by a sheet of glass), the most evocative scene occurs when Thorn returns to his son's birthplace. Wolves are howling, lightning crashing as he uncovers an unhallowed grave, revealing his real son's murdered rotting body, lying beside Damien's real mother... a jackal. Aided and abetted by Jerry Goldsmith's wonderfully bombastic score, full of portent and demonic promise, the film seeks an operatic mood and occasionally achieves it, even if its overly serious tone verges on hysteria.

Damien: Omen II (1978), with teenage Damien now in the care of his uncle, may have suffered in the plot and characterisation departments, but was blessed with the series' most imaginative death scenes. *Omen III: The Final Conflict* (1981) saw Damien as a grown man in a position of growing financial and supernatural power having inherited his family's wealth. A lame TV movie spin-off and a pointless remake in 2006 rounded off the series.

Halloween (1978)

Directed by: John Carpenter
Starring: Jamie Lee Curtis, Donald Pleasence, PJ Soles, Nancy Loomis, Nick Castle

Halloween preparations are being made in Haddonfield and, with most of the adult population apparently out of the area, the older teenagers have to babysit the local kids. Laurie is one such entrepreneurial spirit but, unlike her friends Annie and Lynda, does take her job seriously. They, on the other hand, would much rather be making out with their hunky boyfriends. Sadly, they have made the wrong lifestyle decision as their unbridled sexual fumblings have awakened murderous memories in The Shape, Michael Myers, of a night when he killed his canoodling sister. And tonight is the night he comes home...

The template for many horrors to come, the teen-friendly, mythical *Halloween* epitomises the pinnacle of low-budget inventive filmmaking. The success of any horror film can be measured by the effectiveness of its villain and *Halloween* goes to extraordinary lengths to convince you that there is not a shred of humanity left in Michael Myers, the purpose of which is to create a bogeyman. His nemesis Loomis is crucial too. While his character is ultimately useless in apprehending Myers, he is essential in imparting information to the audience and characters. Laurie is unwittingly thrust into the role of heroine, the virtuous teenager who survives the carnage, which led to criticisms about the reactionary nature of slasher films: the virtuous get to live while the 'bad' deviant teenagers die horribly. The deaths here are spooky rather than bloody – Myers leaving the corpse of one victim, strangled with a telephone cord, spreadeagled on her bed with the tombstone of his dead sister propped up behind her head. That The Shape disappears at the film's close confirms Myers' position as a mythical entity – at once scary (he's still at large) but easily dismissed (clearly he is just a bogeyman). *Halloween* went on to break box-office records; the $325,000 investment saw returns topping $50 million. Absolutely peerless in terms of suspense and technique, *Halloween* redefined the acceptable face of horror.

Director John Carpenter capitalised on his success as the master of modern scares in a succession of finely-paced genre films, including the campfire spook tale *The Fog* (1980), the inventively gory *The Thing* (1982), the Nigel Kneale-inspired *Prince of Darkness* (1987) and the revolutionarily postmodern *In the Mouth of Madness* (1995).

The Evil Dead (1982)

Directed by: Sam Raimi
Starring: Bruce Campbell

Two guys, three girls. A holiday cabin in the countryside. Cut off from civilisation by a rickety bridge, the surrounding woods are host to a mightily evil entity that you really, really wouldn't want to summon, certainly not with an incantation gleaned from a spooky tape recorder and a human-leather-bound book. Ooops...

Funded by hawking the idea to local businessmen, the entrepreneurial spirit and sheer persistence of Raimi and his crew is commendable. The camerawork alone puts many multi-million dollar films to shame, dashing around like a thing possessed, swooping over cars and around trees, smashing through windows and doors. In realising an unstoppable force, the viewer's vantage point goes beyond that of the voyeur usually associated with horror cinema; there is no cut from the prowl to the attack, the watcher becomes as possessed as the characters. Not content with blistering camerawork, Raimi fills his frame with bizarre angles and distorted cartoon figures of fear. The sound is uniformly superb throughout, normally the big let down of low-budget films, with effective use of eerie slowed-down tape and indescribable moans. When the group start turning into cackling, demonically-possessed killers things really start hotting up. Fortunately for gorehounds they can only be dispatched by 'total bodily dismemberment', so heads are lopped off with spades, bodies chainsawed and all manner of gleeful atrocities sloshed about – including a particularly wince-inducing pencil to the ankle. *The Evil Dead* proved problematic for censors because it is so well made that the comic and fantastical elements aren't as noticeable initially as the outrageous violence.

Sam Raimi followed his debut with *Evil Dead 2: Dead By Dawn* (1987) emphasising *Three Stooges*-style comedy mixed with overt gore, which makes it less edgy but a lot of fun. In particular, Campbell's performance becomes hyperactive to the point of insanity, especially when facing his own homicidal possessed hand. The third film, *Army of Darkness* (1992), saw Ash battling his evil self in a mythic world and was played almost entirely for laughs. Raimi's *Darkman* (1990) consolidated his EC horror aesthetic into the superhero genre, while the decidedly low-key gothic of *The Gift* (2000) demonstrated that he was perfectly capable of more restrained filmmaking.

Q: The Winged Serpent (1982)

Directed by: Larry Cohen
Starring: Michael Moriarty, Candy Clark, David Carradine, Richard Roundtree

Prolific writer, director and producer Larry Cohen's astonishing output of 'exploitation' films belies his underlying sense of satire, social commentary and an uncanny ear for dialogue. He has created some of the silver screen's more unusual nemeses, from the killer babies of his *It's Alive* trilogy (1974, 1978, 1987), the mutating dessert anti-consumerist *The Stuff* (1985) to the classic B-monster movie *Q: The Winged Serpent. Q* is a deranged amalgam of genre tropes – detectives investigating a series of bizarre murders, a mysterious human sacrifice cult and, of course, the monster movie. The monster in question is Quetzalcoatl, an Aztec God let loose in New York, summoned by priests who carry out horrific sacrifices on willing victims. The nigh-on unpronounceable winged beast rips a lecherous window cleaner's head off, plucks yuppies from their roof-top pools and enjoys snacking on gangsters fed to it by jittery pianist Jimmy Quinn. Jimmy, you see, knows Quetzalcoatl's whereabouts, a nest atop the Empire State Building, and is quite happy blackmailing the authorities who need this information as the death-toll rises and the streets are showered with human remains.

Despite the links to Herschell Gordon Lewis's *Blood Feast* (1963), *Q*'s greatest homage is to *King Kong*, twisting the climactic scenes at the iconic Empire State Building. Cohen wastes no time in getting the action going – there are three deaths and a bodged jewellery robbery before you've had time to think, along with a scene in a bar that links most of the characters in a way more elegant than in any Michael Mann film. Cohen even uses his budget to his advantage, having Q attack 'into the sun' so that the victims (and the viewers) only catch glimpses of the beast, or it appears as a shadow cast across New York's skyscrapers. When the beast is fully revealed its stop-motion antics only add to the charm. With gore galore, crisp dialogue and a unique monster, *Q* is a B-movie treat of the highest order.

A Nightmare On Elm Street (1984)

Directed by: Wes Craven
Starring: Johnny Depp, Ronnee Blakley, Nick Corri, Robert Englund

Nancy, Tina, Glen and Rod are having nightmares, really bad ones that seem to warp their waking reality, even causing some of them to die in their sleep, screaming in agony. Nancy begins to realise that dreams can come true and uncovers the razor-bladed hand behind the nightmares – multiple child murderer Freddy Krueger, burnt to death by a posse of the town's parents, but now apparently at large again...

Another of Wes Craven's memorable creations, *A Nightmare on Elm Street* and its central ghoul Freddy inadvertently defined the face of 1980s teen horror. Freddy's appeal has a lot to do with his iconic

costume – the dirty green and red sweater, the hat and, most importantly, the razor-endowed glove, whose manufacture we watch during
the film's opening credits. Freddy is a sadist. A child killer. Craven's script
combines the inevitability of succumbing to sleep (*Invasion of the Body
Snatchers* style) with the savagery of a serial slayer. It's an inspired
move: the victims must sleep eventually and, with increasing fatigue,
the blurring between reality and dreamtime becomes more pronounced.
These dream sequences make the whole film one extended set piece,
phasing in and out of alternative realities. As Glen succumbs to sleep
while watching TV on his bed, he is pulled into the mattress by Freddy's
hands and moments later ejected as an eruption of gore that splashes
across the ceiling as his terrified mother watches. Craven never relents
– spooky kid's rhymes, half-grasped horrors and stilted whispers of
ghastly secrets pepper the corners of this influential film.

For over 35 years Wes Craven has been associated with the horror
genre, gaining notoriety with the shockers *Last House on the Left* (1972)
and *The Hills Have Eyes* (1977). He approaches his material with a
psychological and surrealist sensibility that is at odds with much of
mainstream film production. In *Shocker* (1989), a standard, prison-based
serial killer film is transformed into a free-wheeling technologically based
ghost story, while *The People Under the Stairs* (1991) explores social
and racial issues through the eyes of a child, witnessing cannibalism and
worse… Willing to take risks with his material, Craven's films are always
interesting but the finished results can be mixed.

The Toxic Avenger (1985)

Directed by: Michael Herz, Lloyd Kaufman
Starring: Andree Maranda, Mitchell Cohen

Until *The Toxic Avenger*, Kaufman (the manic one) and Herz (the quiet
one) had made predominantly teen sex comedies and distributed a
number of low-budget horror films. *The Toxic Avenger* is an inspired

merging of the two strands – a jubilant, knowingly crass, carnival of two-dimensional characterisation and B-movie splatter. Clumsy geek Melvin mops up at the Tromaville Health Club where rich, hedonistic 'beautiful people' tone their bodies and plan cruel escapades. Melvin is duped into embracing a lingerie-clad sheep while dressed in a pink tutu, but escapes through a window, only to fall into some toxic waste. Burnt, radioactive, disfigured and despised he becomes The Toxic Avenger, a new breed of superhero.

The sheer audacity of Kaufman's bizarre worldview is what makes his bargain-basement films work; their energy and raw insanity ensure a wacky amalgamation of *Porky's* (1982) and *Dawn of the Dead* by way of Fellini and Marvel comics. It could be argued that *The Toxic Avenger* is a fervently left-wing satire on American consumerism, the cult of the beautiful rich and a plea for environmental consciousness. Then again the characters are so completely outrageous that maybe it isn't. Toxie's tormentors get their kicks killing pedestrians, *Death Race 2000* style. They are so evil that, when they only maim a child on a pushbike, they return to reverse over his head so that it splits open like a melon (actually it was a melon), photographing the carnage to ogle at their leisure. The more overt criminals are more outlandish than a 1960s Batman cartoon, but all of them receive exceptionally grizzly comeuppances – eyes poked out, hands thrust into deep fat fryers, burnt, shot, heads squished in gym equipment or shoved in a pizza oven. This vigilante behaviour, each time concluded with the (still tutu-clad) Toxie shoving a mop in the perpetrator's mouth, seems extreme, but in the cartoon world of *The Toxic Avenger*, where the little man can stand up to the corporate fat cats and heart is more important than looks, it seems, well, normal.

Society (1989)

Directed by: Brian Yuzna
Starring: Billy Warlock, Charles Lucia, Patrice Jennings, Ben Slack

In the midst of the late-1980s glut of wise-cracking pantomime villains killing ultra-rich fashionable kids with dated mullet hairstyles, a few teen horrors bucked the trend – Bob Balaban's sublime dissection of the nuclear family *Parents* (1989), Wes Craven's *The People Under the Stairs* (1991) and Brian Yuzna's *Society*. *Society* revels in the staples of the genre before debasing it – even the film's ostensible hero Bill is a product of the boom years. But Bill is different from the rest of his social-climbing family, using his youthful freedom to escape for a life of beach-bound bliss. His parents and sister are, however, part of the upward social network, incestuously happy but vaguely sinister. When a friend warns Bill of a conspiracy between his parents and their powerful friends he becomes paranoid about who he can trust, until finally he unravels a terrifying truth.

If *Society* is a bit too open about the way that the rich and influential literally, as well as figuratively, feed upon the poor then consider it a welcome two-finger salute to an increasingly reactionary genre. Yuzna's film shows the American aristocracy as a race distinct from their plebeian servants and even, it appears, siblings – using privilege as a way of subjugating the proletariat so that they become a mere commodity. In the film's outrageous climax, Bill is captured by his own parents at a society event and shown the excesses of the upper classes. All realised by Screaming Mad George (who is credited with Surrealistic Make-Up Effects), the scene is set for an orgiastic prosthetic *tour de force* unlike any other – bodies contort, faces merge with appendages, people are devoured and assimilated into a miasma of fleshy wanton abandon, their limbs fused with each other in a sweaty cannibalistic frenzy.

Yuzna's work, primarily as a producer, has often given the horror genre a left-field view but has never shied away from the elements that make it so successful with a mass audience.

The Silence of the Lambs (1991)

Directed by: Jonathan Demme
Starring: Jodie Foster, Anthony Hopkins

Forget the lamentable *Hannibal* (2001) and cast from your mind the oft-lauded *Manhunter* (1986), which, despite uniformly superb perform-ances, suffers from pretensions and a seriously poor soundtrack. *The Silence of the Lambs* remains the finest outlet for Thomas Harris's most famous creation. Partly this is because, for most of the running time, Hannibal 'The Cannibal' Lecter remains behind bars, leaving the film to hinge on the more down-to-earth Clarice Starling. Still a rookie, Clarice is given the onerous task of constructing a psychological profile of serial killer Buffalo Bill by eliciting the aid of the incarcerated Lecter. Bill's *modus operandi* is to imprison girls before killing them, then skinning the bodies for his sexual gratification. Demme makes the film memorably horrific by depicting Bill's victims as bodies reduced to butcher's shop carcasses left rotting in the sun, their flayed flesh mainly shown through glimpses of police procedural photographs, far removed from the cartoonish excesses of *Hannibal*.

The *sang froid* shown by the police is almost as chilling as the crimes themselves with only the novice Clarice showing any humanity towards the victims. Instead, the film implicitly blames complacency as the reason for the proliferation of serial killers – two guards are brutally murdered by the apparently trussed-up Hannibal as he breaks free of his confines and escapes the authorities. Accompanied by Tak Fujimoto's effortlessly naturalistic cinematography *The Silence of the Lambs* lends credibility to a contrived but entertaining man-as-monster slasher film that thrills even as it purports to thoughtfully provoke. This marked the beginning of a trend for making the slasher film a respectable genre by imbuing it with the veneer of intellectualism – see, for example, *Copycat* (1995), *The Bone Collector* (1999), *Zodiac* (2007), or any number of similarly macabre police procedural films.

Scream (1996)

Directed by: Wes Craven
Starring: Neve Campbell, David Arquette, Courtney Cox, Drew Barrymore

Sidney is being stalked by a local killer who has already dispatched two of her schoolmates. Still, being a virgin does mean that she is qualified to survive the film, as geeky genre aficionado Randy is quick to point out. What the kids need to cheer themselves up is a party, a cathartic horror film and a reiteration of the three basic rules about teenage slasher flicks – don't have sex, don't do drugs and never, ever say 'I'll be right back'.

The teen slasher flick had taken a serious nose-dive in the 1990s due to tightening censorship regulations on both sides of the pond and a formula that had run itself dry. Enter Wes Craven and young scriptwriter Kevin Williamson who between them resurrected the corpse of the genre and introduced the stalk and slash film to a new generation. Knowingly iconic, deeply ironic, the killer wears a billowing black cape and a mask that mirrors Munch's *The Scream* from which the film derives its title. *Scream* owes a huge debt to its predecessors but doesn't compromise what made them so popular in the first place. The decline of the horror film was partly due to the sneering attitude that lazy producers took to the product: the endless sequels and the shallow comedy. *Scream* remains a comedy and a quiz game but never balks when it comes to the scares and the gore – there are multiple stabbings, entrails roll and one student is discovered, part-bisected, having tried to escape through a cat-flap. It never takes itself seriously and, while the revelations are suitably *Scooby Doo,* it remains a genuinely 'Scary Movie'.

The Sixth Sense (1999)

Directed by: M Night Shyamalan
Starring: Bruce Willis, Haley Joel Osment, Toni Collette

Shot by one of his patients, Vincent, child psychologist Dr Malcolm Crowe no longer feels confident about his work and his marriage is definitely in poor shape. His only chance at exorcising his demons lies with a new patient, Cole Sear, a highly disturbed child whose case is almost identical to that of Vincent's. The boy suffers from intense and frequent hallucinations: solid, real depictions of the walking dead, people whose spirits are not at rest and are doomed to roam in eternal limbo unless their malcontent is resolved.

The horror in *The Sixth Sense* lies with a child, an innocent, being subjected to forces that no child should know. The lack of complicity or reasoning behind Cole's affliction merely adds to the brooding sense of unease that pervades Shyamalan's quiet film. It is more unnerving than outright scary, with young Haley Joel Osment giving a convincing and desperate performance as Cole, his wide eyes gazing with futile inevitability at another silent, mutilated ghost. Willis, too, handles his role with surprising sensitivity; as he slowly drifts away from his wife, deteriorating into a spiral of despair and regret, his only salvation lies in Cole's hands. The film's pace is languid, preferring to reserve any shock tactics for a few key scenes. Cinematographer Tak Fujimoto shoots the film with a grimy 1970s feel, his camera gliding for minutes without cutting, absorbing the viewer into a believable and non-jarring environment. The film engrosses rather then assaults. Writer/director M Night Shyamalan never falls into the trap of deliberate gross-out, and even 'that' ending is handled almost matter-of-factly and is far better for it, although his subsequent films – *Unbreakable* (2000), *Signs* (2002) and *The Village* (2004) – would suffer from audience expectations of a 'big twist'.

Final Destination (2000)

Directed by: James Wong
Starring: Devon Saw, Ali Larter, Kristen Cloke, Seann William Scott

In terms of the serial killer or supernatural death film *Final Destination* is its *reductio ad absurdum par excellence*. No psychological traumas turning a child into a psychopath, no witchcraft, no vengeful spirits. In the high-concept world of *Final Destination* the cause of death is Death, and not even a scythe-wielding skeletal figure, just Death itself. A school trip to France is scuppered when Alex gets a premonition of disaster, freaks out and, along with six others, is turfed off the plane. When his premonitions come true and it explodes mid-air killing all aboard he is viewed with suspicion, especially when, one by one, the survivors suffer a series of increasingly messy deaths.

Final Destination's lack of backstory and patently absurd death scenes are what make it such an enjoyable film. Because they have cheated by escaping the aircrash, the survivors are picked off in the order they were due to die ensuring that Death's big book of souls balances at the end of the fiscal year. But Death doesn't just smite them or arrange discreet heart attacks, oh no; instead an elaborate and convoluted series of vaguely supernaturally enhanced accidents dispatch the unfortunate victims. Often accompanied by an ominous wind or inexplicable lightning, some of the deaths are heavily signposted to elicit tension, others are deliberately sudden sleights of hand that provide jolts of surprise. The only surviving school teacher suffers a protracted and hilarious series of mishaps offering 101 different death possibilities, eventually succumbing to a bewildering melange of fates including burning, stabbing and an almighty explosion. Unadulterated, unapologetic hokum designed to spill your popcorn in fright and make you laugh like a hyena afterwards, horror aficionados can also have fun spotting the references in the characters' names – Billy Hitchcock, Larry Murnau, even Val(erie) Lewton!

Ginger Snaps (2000), Canada

Directed by: John Fawcett
Starring: Emily Perkins, Katharine Isabelle, Kris Lemche, Mimi Rogers

Although there have been female werewolves before (notably *The Howling* [1981]) the majority of werewolf movies concentrate on the male's lack of control as a metaphor for sexual desire or as a pack film with a metamorphosing mythological edge. *Ginger Snaps*, however, concerns itself with lycanthropy as a metaphor for blossoming female desires in a contemporary context, the confusion of growing up and youth's inherent nihilism. The Fitzgerald sisters, Brigitte and Ginger, are suicide-obsessed adolescents and the butt of many high-school jokes. The girls are introduced via their hobby in which they feign their own increasingly gruesome suicides and photograph the results. Following a series of incidents where local dogs have been ripped to pieces, the pair decide to fake the death of premier bitch Trina Sinclair's prize pooch, only for the plan to go horribly wrong when they stumble across the real perpetrator – a snarling grey beast that slashes Ginger before being mown down by the van of their neighbourhood drug-dealer. Ginger becomes infected, turning into a werewolf and developing a liking for dominant sex and fresh flesh.

Unlike many of the cycle in postmodern horrors, *Ginger Snaps* wears its genre knowledge with more subtlety, twisting conventions (no silver bullets, no on-off transformations) but never to breaking point. Similarly the issues the picture raises about teenage suicide, menstruation, drugs and high-school conflicts add to the realism rather than signpost their liberal feminism. In effect, this is *Heathers* with lycanthropes and dead dogs – a tense, gory but topical film about female isolation in suburbia that doesn't balk on the viscera and never ladles its liberalism.

Hostel (2005)

Directed by: Eli Roth
Starring: Jay Hernandez, Derek Richardson, Eythor Gudjonsson

After his debut, the gore-drenched love-letter to 1970s horror films *Cabin Fever* (2002), *Hostel* is Roth's twist on the political-subtext horror, questioning America's role on the world stage. Two Americans and their Icelandic companion party in Amsterdam before heading to Slovakia in search of loose women and cheap booze. But they don't realise that the hostel is a front for a lucrative business that allows rich clients to torture and kill for fun… and they are next in line.

Were it not for the opening shots of flesh and blood being casually washed down a drain you could be forgiven for thinking that this is not a horror film but a hedonistic stoner romp around Europe. But Roth is playing with audience expectations, giving us a chance to empathise with the protagonists, particularly the signposted 'good' boy. That he doesn't end up being the final boy but just another slab of meat is one of the many twists that make *Hostel* so gut-wrenching but also filled with gallows humour. Once *Hostel* has established its warehouse of death the film never lets go, becoming a gruelling ride of desperation, torture and pain. In one scene the victim is given the chance to leave, save for the fact his tendons have been severed and he is unable even to crawl. A Japanese girl is found, her face burned with a blowtorch, her right eye flopping around on her cheek. In order to stop her agony they cut the eye off, a squirt of pus trickling down her scarred face. Later, unable to cope with the mutilation she throws herself in front of a train. This is one of many nods to Japanese horror (J-horror), here *Suicide Club* (2002), and there's also a cameo from cult bad-boy Miike Takashi. What sets *Hostel* apart from other recent gore-flicks is that it has the confidence to build up its characterisation before launching into the atrocities, making its unflinching violence far more potent.

Central and South American Horror Cinema

The Lumière Brothers sent their representatives far and wide to tell the world about their new invention of cinema. Two groups were sent to Latin America – one to Rio de Janeiro, Buenos Aires and Montevideo and the other group to Mexico and Havana. Of these it was only really Mexico, Argentina and Brazil that managed to kickstart their film industries, with large enough audiences to justify film production costs. A number of silent films were made, mainly by aficionados and on comparatively low budgets, and many were imported; hence German Expressionist films and some US horrors made their way into the cinemas of South Amercia. It was Hollywood that tried to force Latin American cinemas to convert to sound, recognising the vast potential for sales across the continent. They did this initially by making Spanish-language versions of their own productions, the most notable horror film of which was the Spanish version of Tod Browning's *Dracula* (1931). George Melford shot the film back-to-back with the English-language version – Bela Lugosi portrayed Dracula during the daytime, then Carlos Villarias took over to play the role using the same sets at night. The experiment wasn't commercially successful, though, partly because of the actors' dialects, which confused audiences.

Film as an artform really took hold in Mexico in the mid-1930s and, with funding from the government and the formation of the first film union, production increased dramatically in genres as far ranging as melodramas and rancheras, films analogous to the Western. Horror was a genre that definitely appealed to Mexicans and, although the language of cinema was still developing, a number of different local styles developed. Local legends often formed the basis for stories. *La Llorona* (*The Crying Woman*, 1933) tells three tales, two in flashback, each relating to the tragic and violent loss of a child. La Llorona became a character that would appear in a number of future Mexican productions, most notably in Rafael Baledón's *La Maldición de La Llorona* (1963).

Juan Bustillo Oro was one of Mexico's better-known writer/directors and often considered to be the father of Mexican horror. *Dos Monjes* (*Two Monks*, 1934) told the tale of two friends who fell in love with the same woman and became monks after she was killed. Filmed from the viewpoints of each lover this drama explores the themes of twisted love and the nature of trust. Oro made many films in a variety of genres over the years, frequently penning them himself, including *El Misterio del rostro pálido* (*The Mystery of the Terrible Face*, 1935) and what is perhaps his most famous work *El Hombre sin rostro* (1950) in which a detective has terrifying dreams of a faceless woman which he associates with his quest to uncover the secret behind a horrific murder.

Apart from a few productions in the 1940s, horror declined until the 1950s when an inspired idea to revitalise the genre came along in a manner unique to Mexico. Mexicans had long been fond of watching Lucha Libre – professional wrestling – on the television. Although undoubtedly a sport, it had the capacity to develop the wrestlers' larger-than-life characters – good guys and bad guys – and storylines for the combatants. By mixing this popular format with fantasy and supernatural characters, a new genre was born with the usually masked wrestlers creating alter ego superhero personas. El Santo (The Saint, real name Rodolfo Guzman Huerta) was the undisputed king of the cinema ring. Initially a bad guy, he turned to the side of good and saw his star ascend in his first classic picture *Santo contra los zombies* (*Santo vs the Zombies*) in 1961. Santo is both a wrestler and crimefighter who occasionally has to dash off to fight a quick wrestling bout before returning to solve the crime and dispatch the bad guys. Occasionally teaming up with The Blue Demon, Santo wrestled many, many opponents, including witches, vampires, wolfmen, mummies, mad scientists, zombies and even Frankenstein's daughter. His son, El Hijo del Santo, has carried on the Santo name and has also appeared in films.

In the meantime, a number of more traditional horror productions had infiltrated Mexican audiences, particularly those with supernatural and mad scientist themes. Some of the best of these films included Chano Urueta's *El monstruo resucitado* (1953), which features actor José María Linares-Rivas as a plastic surgeon who brings a corpse back to life, and *La bruja* (1954), in which a hideous hag is transformed into a luscious lady by a scientist, although her new-found beauty really is only skin deep. Urueta also directed *El Barón del terror* (1962), aka *Brainiac*, a bizarre and somewhat outrageous tale of a Baron who dies at the hands of the Inquisition, only to return many years later as a brain-eating monster. Aztec Mummies were popular too and featured in a number of films including *La Momia azteca* and *La Maldición de la momia azteca* in 1957 and the gleefully messy *La Momia azteca contra el robot humano* (*Robot vs The Aztec Mummy*, 1958). The series ran until the late 1960s.

In 1957, Fernando Méndez made *Ladrón de cadavers*, a wrestling film where one of the combatants is given a brain transplant from a gorilla. Enormously popular, it led producer (and future *Brainiac* star) Abel Salazar to commission Méndez to make what would becomes his most famous film, *El Vampiro* (1957), starring Germán Robles as a smooth, suave count. A sequel soon followed – *El ataud del vampiro* (*The Vampire's Coffin*, 1958) – as well as a number of other monster movies from Salazar's production company.

Mexico experienced its golden age of cinema between 1953 and 1965 but there were still a number of directors working in the genre in later years, although some stayed far away from the mainstream. Chilean-born Alejandro Jodorowsky had travelled the world before arriving in Mexico in the 1960s. Involved with many art forms, but with an overall love of cinema and strong penchant for the extreme *avant garde*, he was involved in the theatre before directing *Fando y Lis* (1968), a film which was banned by the Mexican government. Never afraid to court controversy, it told the story of Fando and his disabled girlfriend Lis and their journey to find a mystical city. One scene features a decadent man who drinks Lis' blood, but does so by extracting it from her arm into a glass – after all, one has to have standards and observe etiquette when it comes to exploiting the lower classes. Jodorowsky went on to make *El Topo*

(1970), an underground allegorical Western (sort of) about a gunfighter seeking enlightenment that's notable for its sense of intense surreal brutality. *La Montaña Sagrada* (*The Holy Mountain*, 1973) followed, and various aborted projects. *Santa Sangre* (1989) is his most accessible work and still imbued with elements of the fantastical that mark it as far outside mainstream cinema. Jodorowsky has continued to make films, albeit sporadically, but all bearing his unique, if twisted, vision.

Juan López Moctezuma had spent some time working with Jodorowsky before launching his directorial debut *El Mansion de la locura* (1973), using his mentor's themes of madness, violence and those outside of society in a bizarre film about torture, forced slaughter and depravity in an asylum run by the insane Dr Tarrs. He followed with the vampire film *Mary, Bloody Mary* (1975), featuring John Carradine as the father vampire of bisexual bloodsucker Mary. Perhaps his best-known work is *Alucarda, la hija de las tinieblas* (*Sisters of Satan*, 1978).

Guillermo del Toro was born in Guadalajara and adored horror films as a child. He worked in television and made two shorts, *Doña Lupe* (1985) and *Geometria* (1987), before finding the funding to make his debut feature *Cronos* (1992). Its huge critical success led to del Toro being snapped up by Hollywood. However, he remains loyal to his roots and tends to alternate between making large Hollywood productions (*Mimic* [1997], *Blade 2* [2002], *Hellboy* [2004]) and smaller Spanish-language films (the genuinely unnerving *Devil's Backbone* [2001] and the delightful but savage *Pan's Labyrinth* [2006]), the latter of which are more satisfying in their consistent worldview. All his films bear a marked authorial stamp, particularly an obsession with the innocence of child-hood, arcane clockwork machinery and the ubiquity of insects. Visually his work is an astounding blend of the fantastical and the nostalgic, always ravishing to the eyes, even during the most gruelling of scenes – something he manages to get across in the PG-13 superhero horror *Hellboy*.

Aside from Mexico's love of genre, there were no defined horror trends that developed elsewhere in South America. However, there were a few filmmakers who devoted themselves to the cause, including Argentina's prolific Emilio Vierya who made a number of low-budget horrors in the 1960s and 70s, all replete with copious quantities of sex. Actor Narsisco Ibanez Menta was a huge fan of Lon Chaney and appeared in the Argentinian horror anthology *Obras maestras del terror* (1960). Generally though, Argentina is a country more concerned with serious or political films than macabre fantasies, partly as a result of its turbulent history.

Brazil has had a long cinema history that reached its peak in the 1960s and has recently come to prominence on the world cinematic stage through such excellent socio-political dramas as *City of God* (2002) and *Central Station* (1998). One of the more distinctive of horror directors is undoubtedly Brazilian José Mojica Marins, also known as Zé do Caixão or Coffin Joe[9]. Played by an utterly self-confident Marins, Zé do Caixão is a caped, top-hatted sadist and torturer with exceptionally long finger-nails, a seemingly unstoppable invocation of the id run riot in a society of Catholic convention. His debut feature *À Meia-Noite Levarei Sua Alma* (*At Midnight I'll Steal Your Soul,* 1964) dived straight in with shocking imagery. If the basic trappings of the horror film are familiar – Zé do Caixão wants a bride, he menaces the local town, order is restored at the close – *At Midnight I'll Steal Your Soul* exceeds expectations in the manner of its portrayal. A sequel, *Esta Noite Encarnarei no Teu Cadáver* (1967), followed. If Zé's early films were horrors that implicitly challenged society, *O Despertar da Besta* (*Awakening of the Beast,* 1970) was an explicit condemnation of society's decline in moral standards and the authorities' inability to confront pressing issues. At times the effect on the viewer is as disorientating as the drugs taken by the denizens of the crumbling society portrayed. *Awakening of the Beast* was not cut by the censors, it was banned outright, and Marins' career suffered as a result. Although some of the unrestrained personal glee sneaked through in later projects such as *Finis Hominis* (*The End of Man,* 1971), *O Exorcismo Negro (The Bloody Exorcism of Coffin Joe,* 1974) and *Perversão* (*Perversion,* 1979), they were more projects for hire. A far cry from the halcyon days of the 1960s when Zé do Caixão, a figure kept in the public eye not just on film but through television and even comic books, held Brazil in the tangled claws of his spiralling fingernails.

The fantastic is part of the national culture in Latin America – each year has a Day of the Dead celebration, a festival of remembrance for departed loved ones, filled with bright and macabre imagery. However, as a result of the turbulent politics of the twentieth century, which saw revolutions, dictatorships and coups d'état, the film industries of the respective countries, often subject to state control, struggled to maintain a consistent output, and only Mexico managed to realise a popular horror movement. However, with Brazil and Argentina in particular producing world-class cinema, perhaps it won't be long before this situation changes.

El Vampiro (1957), Mexico

Directed by: Fernando Méndez
Starring: Germán Robles

Count Karol de Lavud's suave, impeccably dressed vampire is the towering presence of menace in this hugely influential reworking of *Dracula*. Indeed it would be hard to imagine Frank Langella's version of the count without him. Plucky Marta returns to her family home, meeting the overly jovial Enrique on the way. Enrique is an undercover agent for Marta's uncle, here to explain the mysterious deaths that have plagued the locals and family, as well as neighbourly aristocrat Mr Duvel's attempts to purchase the decrepit hacienda. Duvel is also not who he seems. He is Count Karol de Lavud and currently draining the local villagers in order to resurrect his long-dead brother and desperate to turn Marta into a vampire, like her black-clad aunt.

Before the credits have opened we have already seen the Count in action, transforming into a bat and sucking blood, a portent of things to come. Although the trappings of the early Universal films are apparent in the set-up, *El Vampiro* defies the linear nature of a standard *Dracula* homage, revealing each of its characters' multiple personalities and disguises as the film progresses. Particularly striking are the in-camera transformations of the Count into a vampire bat, achieved via perfectly timed jumpcuts and careful editing, making him explicitly a figure of supernatural fear. When we see him savaging a peasant led to her death by the vampiric aunt, he emerges from the coat and transforms into a bat, dive bombing his victim with such ferocity that her hat shoots off. Gnawing at her neck he transforms back into his human form, smothering her with his cloak as he drains the last vestiges of life from her frail body. Méndez piles on the atmosphere in the scenes of cobweb-covered crypts and ghostly appearances. A familiar tale told with enough twists to make it fresh, combined with inventive effects, atmospheric visuals and an aristocratically dominant central vampire, make *El Vampiro* a defining film in Mexican and vampire cinema.

Esta Noite Encarnarei no Teu Cadáver (This Night I Will Possess Your Corpse) (1967), Brazil

Directed by and starring: José Mojica Marins

Zé do Caixão had received his comeuppance at the end of *At Midnight I Will Take Your Soul* but, in the tradition of horror franchises, this denouement is conveniently ignored and he initiates a quest to find a 'superior woman' to be his bride. He aims to create the perfect being – the progeny of the superman. Zé's goal is realised by terrorising scantily clad women with tarantulas or poisonous snakes to determine who has the most fortitude. Zé is a figure of fear primarily because he does not feel confined by any sense of moral or social constraint – he is as 'superior' as he thinks he is precisely because he has unilaterally decided to flaunt society's rigidity and expectations. The greatest fear is that of divine retribution either in this life or, more usually accepted, in the afterlife.

Zé's hubris and blasphemy mean that he not only lacks the

restraining hand of religious orthodoxy, he openly defies it. His orgies of violence are unprovoked and therefore make his position untenable, so his transgressions must inevitably be punished. *This Night I Will Possess Your Corpse* is filled to the brim with breathtaking images and flights of imagination. In the film's most celebrated sequence Zé do Caixão's first stirrings of faith and doubt bring on an astonishing hallucination. Dragged from his slumbering bride by an almost impossibly thin black demon, he's taken to the graveyard where disembodied hands burst forth from their graves and pull him to Hell. In stark contrast to the monochrome life on earth, Hell is a garish landscape of piercing primary colour, jarring the senses into overload. Successions of screaming naked bodies are flogged, beaten and cajoled by imps. Body parts twitch from the walls and torrents of blood are accompanied by the despairing moans of the damned. These vignettes are worthy of Bruegel or Bosch in what marks Marins' most astonishing depiction of the torments of sinners.

Alucarda, la hija de las tinieblas (1978), Mexico

Directed by: Juan López Moctezuma
Starring: Tina Romero, Susana Kamini

'Satan, Satan, Satan, our lord and master. I acknowledge thee as my lord and prince.'

Mexico is a predominantly Catholic country and *Alucarda* a prime example of the religious exploitation film in which the eternal torment that faces non-believers is revealed by allowing us the privilege of witnessing their wickedness. Featuring some truly imaginative use of lighting to create an otherworldly environment and arresting images that linger in the mind, *Alucarda* tells its story of Satanism and life after death in a fantastical and exploitative context. Justine shares her new convent home with the striking but strange Alucarda, who demands that Justine love her to death. Alucarda knows all about the beauty beyond death and has no qualms running off to look at gypsy charms with the oddly bearded hunchback or planning elaborate revenge on the world in general when possessed by the demon Asteroth. What takes *Alucarda* from the realms of the standard exploitation flick – there's lots of nudity and Kensington Gore on show here – is the elaborate use of imagery to nail home its point, right down to the multitudes of twisted Christ figures that surround the 'fire and brimstone' priest as he lectures on the torments of Hell. *Alucarda*'s grand finale shows the final links between the forces of the church, science and the devil in that their actions only ever seem to result in the destruction of innocence. The astonishing pyrokinetic showdown is replete with religious symbolism juxtaposing the flaming Christ with the apocalyptic carnage engulfing the nunnery, all carefully photographed by cinematographer Xavier Cruz. A film then that has its cake and eats it, showing us the evils of the devil so we can delight in refuting it.

Santa Sangre (1989), Mexico

Directed by: Alejandro Jodorowsky
Starring: Axel Jodorowsky, Blanca Guerra, Sabrina Dennison

Alejandro Jodorowsky's brutal and beautiful films have often walked the fine line between art and exploitation, profound and pretentious. *Santa Sangre* defies the simple explanation that it is a glorified giallo with arthouse pretensions. Jodorowsky's son Axel plays Fenix, an acrobatic and disturbed adult whose life story as a circus performer is revealed in flashback. This is a grandiose film of extremes. Fenix's knife-throwing father binds him to a chair and tattoos an eagle on his chest, then later cuts off his mother Concha's arms after she throws acid on his genitals for his infidelities. *Santa Sangre* lives up to its title in many ways. It is bathed in blood from the dying elephant spurting gore from its trunk to the vicious murder of the painted lady who prostitutes Fenix's love, Alma, and the sacred pool of blood in Concha's church. Fenix himself is seen as a Christ-like figure, destined to a life of servitude as his mother's missing arms, performing as 'Concha and her Magic Hands' complete with long and crimson fingernails. His only love is the abused deaf-mute Alma, who silently witnesses the carnage that peppers the film, the true victim of this operatic tragedy.

Bathed in unnatural light, accompanied by Simon Boswell's hypnotic fairground score, *Santa Sangre* is a film that sears into your brain with its surreal and savage imagery, its juxtaposition of life's brutality with the desecration of innocence, a theme best summed up when the violated Alma dreamily walks through the night-time streets as discarded skeleton balloons from the Day of the Dead festival drift serenely past her like spectres on her damaged mind.

Cronos (1992), Mexico

Directed by: Guillermo del Toro
Starring: Federico Luppi, Claudio Brook, Ron Perlman

A sixteenth-century alchemist creates the Cronos device, a clockwork instrument that extends the life of those who use it. Years later, ageing rich businessman De La Guardia and his delinquent offspring Angel seek the mechanism, but it now belongs to Jesus Gris, who runs an antique shop with his granddaughter Aurora. Gris has become addicted to the device, which makes him youthful but also gives him a craving for human blood. Angel unwisely kills Gris, but he returns from beyond the grave and seeks revenge.

This wonderful gothic Mexican horror tale is very quiet and under-played and contains many of the themes that would permeate del Toro's later work. Ultimately it is a film about family love – Aurora knows about the Cronos device and tries to keep it from Gris, but although she doesn't want her grandfather to be an addict, she realises it makes him happy. All would be cosy were it not for two things: Gris's physical state is deteriorating rapidly – he's basically a walking, decomposing corpse –

and De La Guardia's barmy son, played with aplomb by Ron Perlman, who is constantly on his trail. This is a strangely moving film, at times gentle (Aurora is seen preparing bedtime blankets for her animated deceased grandfather), at times morbidly humorous (the memorably eccentric mortician asks whether they want the corpse 'medium rare or well done'), and sometimes a little bit gross (Gris vomits bloods as he adapts to the Cronos device), but it's always original and intriguing.

HORROR IN ASIA

Asia's bewildering array of cultures, religions, customs and languages makes it impossible to document in anything like a comprehensive manner. Rather like Europe, a number of Asian countries generated definable horror movements while others produced only sporadic examples of the genre. In the Philippines, for example, a healthy film industry had thrived prior to World War Two. Indeed the country's first sound film, *Ang Aswang* (1931), is based on a local vampire-like legend featuring a shape-shifting snake woman. This particular monster proved so popular that versions of the story are periodically produced to appeal to each successive generation. Filipino film was vibrant in the 1960s and 1970s, with many filmmakers (for example Eddie Romero) supplementing their income by producing exploitation films for the international market. Currently there is a new movement of Filipino horror beginning to create a wave outside its home territory – the Tagalog film *Sigaw* (aka *Echoes*, 2004), an eerie, haunted-flat film where the spirits invade the lives of its occupants even after they have left the accursed building, has been optioned for a US remake.

Similarly, Thai filmmakers the Pang Brothers (*Bangkok Haunted* [2001], *Ab-normal Beauty* [2004]) have had their hit *The Eye* (1999) remade into English. Although the Thai film industry can be traced back to the beginnings of cinema it was almost decimated by the influx of Hollywood product, until a horror film, Nonzee Nimibutr's *Nang-Nak* (1999), broke box office records and revitalised the industry. A solid market for horror has now been established with films as diverse as the

bizarre 'undead and weapons' film *Curse of the Sun* (2004), the supernatural films *Art of the Devil* (2005) and *Narok* (*Hell*, 2005), and the truly
terrifying ghost film *Shutter* (2004), in which developed photos reveal
glimpses of the supernatural. The well-established Asian horror tropes
are brilliantly offset by character revelations as we begin to realise that
events surrounding an apparent road accident are anything other than
co-incidental.

Indonesia's film industry has had its ups and downs, but it has a long
tradition of scary movies. Although production values are not always
high, the output is largely enjoyable, if a touch bizarre. Often soaked in
gore, frequently dealing with graphic amputations and hideous apparitions of grotesque monsters, the Indonesian horror tradition is often
placed in a fantasy context. The monsters derive from local legends and
magic often forms a major part of the plot. A *penanggalen* is one such
creature, a woman whose head, spinal cord and oesophagus detach
from the rest of her body then fly through the air in search of victims.
The most famous film about these creatures is *Leák* (*Mystics in Bali*,
1981) which tells the tale of an American girl who bites off more than
she can chew whilst investigating the black magic secrets of Bali. Many
other South East Asian countries also have legends about *penanggalen*
as well as *pontianaks* and *langsuyar*, female ghost spirits closely related
to the vampire. A successful series of *pontianak* films were made in
Malaysia – *Pontianak* (1957), *Dendam Pontianak* (1957), *Sumpah
Pontianak* (1958) and *Pontianak Kembali* (1963), and the creature still
crops up in modern productions.

Japanese Horror Cinema

In 1998 Nakata Hideo's low-budget, low-key horror film *Ringu* took the
Japanese box office and eventually the international one by storm.
Spawning sequels as well as remakes in Korea and the US, *Ringu*
became the calling card for contemporary Japanese horror films. In many
ways, thematically *Ringu* is a culmination of Japanese horror tropes that

typified the country's filmmaking over the preceding century. Its international success lay in its back-of-a-postage-stamp simplicity, its universality and its restraint in the gore department. Most importantly, within the confines of a cinema, it is very scary indeed. Japanese horror had been sporadically popular outside the country before, usually with aficionados or on the international art-house circuit, but *Ringu* tapped into a more mainstream consciousness while retaining its Japanese aesthetic and thematic elements. At heart it is a ghost story, or *kaidan* (or *kwaidan*) *monogatari*, but *Ringu* adds the technological twist of linking the traditional *kaidan monogatari* with videotape to create a contemporary tale. As the most technologically advanced and saturated society in the world, Japan nevertheless has a distinctly cautionary approach to science and technology in its films – technology is prosperity but it also represents a debasing of the natural and hence a cause for concern. One of the main religions in Japan, Shinto, is an animistic religion that reinforces the harmonious in nature and sees the spiritual in all things. Shinto not only identifies with the natural order, it also comes with a pantheon of ghosts (*kaidan*), spirits (*yōkai*) and demons (*oni*) that feed directly into fantastical films and literature. This literary and religious heritage has a long lineage and its effects are notable not only in period *kaidan monogatari* such as *Kuroneko* (1968) but also in contemporary cinema. Japan's most famous monster, *Gojira* (*Godzilla*, 1954), is from this tradition. Born out of nuclear bomb testing in the Pacific, he roars his way across Japan, decimating buildings with each mighty reptilian step. He is Shinto vengeance made flesh, nature rebelling against the unbridled progress of technology and the evil of nuclear warfare.

Horror has always been a popular genre in Japan and many horror films are released in the summer months, the chill of the scares providing respite from the heat and humidity that typify the season. The influence of folktales and religious texts on the Japanese horror film is pronounced but so too are the works of writers such as Ueda Akinari and Edogawa Rampo (Hirai Taro, a prolific writer whose *nom de plume* was derived from a transliterated Edgar Allan Poe). More recently, manga artists have provided the inspiration for many films, such as the prolific Ito Junji whose long-running series *Tomie* has provided the basis for a number of films. Some manga artists such as Takashi Ishii (*Freezer, Black Angel, Gonin*) have also become filmmakers. The links between literature, manga and film have never been more integrated and sometimes a story can appear in all these media. *Ringu* started as a novel before being made into a TV movie, a film and a manga. It is a common trait of Japanese cinema that it is part of a wider multimedia product that extends beyond the screen space. This is especially true of the way Japanese film relies on techniques that have been derived from literature and traditional stage productions such as *Noh* or *Kabuki*. Text, prints and oral tradition – silent films in Japan were often accompanied by a narrator (*benshi*) who was sometimes more important to a film's success than the film itself – mean that Japanese cinema is difficult to understand in isolation.

Japan had begun developing its own films in the late nineteenth century, initially adaptations of kabuki plays and traditional stories, including some *kaidan monogatari*. Even in these early films the aesthetic distancing made them distinct from their western counterparts. Sadly a great deal of early film has been destroyed and, in the case of Japan, much prior to 1945 is lost forever after the devastation of World War Two. What remains are secondary sources, contemporary commentary, fragments of footage and stills. So we may never see *The Lasciviousness of the Viper* (1921), an early version of the story that would become Mizoguchi's celebrated *Ugetsu Monogatari* (1953) or *The Living Corpse* (1917). One film that did survive (found in a rice barrel in 1971 in the director's garden shed) is *A Page of Madness* (1926), a hallucinatory tale set in a lunatic asylum, half Soviet montage, half *Cabinet of Doctor Caligari*. In the 1930s and 40s censorship by the increasingly militant government made production difficult for many filmmakers. What was produced tended to be high-quality drama, period pieces or propaganda. The horror film, although not dead, was not in the best of health.

As Japan began its recovery in the postwar years so did its rediscovering of the two strands of horror film – the contemporary (*Gojira*) and the period (*jidaigeki*, such as *Ugetsu Monogatari*). *Gojira*'s bleakness soon metamorphosed into the colourful excess of the monster (*kaiju*) films, which were typified by fantastical battles between massive beasts set against a backdrop of a normally helpless Japan. There was nothing quite like seeing the familiar destroyed in an orgy of orchestrated mayhem, and so cities across the country vied to be decimated by Mothra, Gamera and a whole menagerie of atomic superbeasts. Admittedly what had started as cautionary horror and political metaphor soon descended into a latex-suited wrestling match but the results led to a popularisation of monster culture that would prepare youngsters for the full-blooded horror of the *kaidan monogatari*. Honda Ishiro, the director of the original *Gojira* and long-time friend and collaborator with Kurosawa Akira, would occasionally return to his most famous creation but also produced further horrors such as the underrated psychedelic insanity drama *Matango* (*Matango: Fungus of Terror*, 1963). *Matango* follows the sorry tale of a shipwrecked bunch of misfits trying to survive on an island. Their hunger leads to some of them consuming the local mushrooms with devastating results. *Matango* shows the breakdown of society in microcosm and contrasts the highly saturated colour palette with a bleak vision of humanity that is projected way past the film's final, haunting frames.

Meanwhile, Nakagawa Nobuo was creating more traditional tales. His films, particularly in the 1950s and 1960s, often featured ghosts, castles and misty encounters but within these familiar confines he offered an audience something else – shock. Although he had been directing since 1938, Nakagawa came to attention for a series of films – including *Kaidan Kasane-ga-fuchi* (1957) and *Onna kyuketsuki* (*Bloodsucker Woman*, 1959) – made at the Shin Toho studios when it had begun to move into lower-budget thrill pictures. But it was with *Tokaido Yotsuya kaidan* (1959) and particularly *Jigoku* (1960) that he came to wider international attention, blending familiar scenarios with full-blooded *Grand Guignol*. The effect on Japanese horror was pronounced, and the implied horror of past productions proved to be perfectly adaptable to a new, more visceral aesthetic. Nakagawa continued directing films, though more sporadically and often on television, for the 1970s weren't kind to 'old school' directors, until his final ghost tale *Kaiidan: Ikiteiru Koheiji* (1982). Nakagawa's pioneering work would fuel the Japanese horror picture's desire for experimentation. Sato Hajime used contemporary settings, giving his films a science fiction slant in a series including *Kaitei Daisensô* (*Battle Beneath the Sea*, 1966) and *Kyuketsuki Gokemidoro* (*Goke: Bodysnatcher from Hell*, 1968), a lurid and apocalyptic story of alien invasion set against an eye-searing palette of primary colours.

The 1950s and early 60s were a boom era for the Japanese film industry but, by the 1970s, budgets had been slashed and some studios forced to the brink of ruin. This led to an increase in exploitation product and eventually a thriving straight-to-video market that continues to this day, but without the stigma that it has in the West. An upside of this situation was that filmmakers, depending on what studio they worked with, could have far more freedom when choosing what to shoot as long as it contained sex or violence. Since the 1950s, Japanese cinema has not shied away from depictions of sex, violence and sexualised violence in its productions, despite some apparently arbitrary censorship requirements regarding aspects of nudity. These were not just limited to the lower end of the market. A film such as the explicitly gory *jidaigeki The Joy of Torture: Oxen Split Torturing* (1968) was relatively prestigious despite the excruciating scenes of crucifixion, disembowelment, forced eating of severed body parts and all manner of atrocities. In the less exalted world of the pornographic movie, the free reign offered to directors produced a number of artistic, almost wholly grim films exploring the dark murderous side of sexuality. These included Wakamatsu Koji's *Yuke yuke nidome no shojo* (*Go Go Second Time Virgin*, 1969) and *Okasareta hakui* (*Violated Angels*, 1967), a look into the world of a rapist serial killer modelled on nurse-obsessed Richard Speck.

It was around this time that a fascination for medical horror films began to emerge, perhaps foreshadowed by Masumura Yaszuo's *Akai tenshi* (*The Red Angel,* 1966), a dark and moving sexual drama set during the war. A sub-genre of medical terror has continued to hold a fascination to this day, from schlock gore-fest *Kansen* (*Infection*, 2004) to Fujiwara Kei's incomparably grim *Organ* (1996) and Tsukamoto Shinya's arty autopsy thriller *Vital* (2005). Medical imagery, with its cold, clinical, unrelenting harshness, reflects the love-hate relationship with science and can also be seen in Miike Takashi's wince-inducing slow-burner *Audition* (2000) with its vengeful, syringe-wielding, rubber-gloved mutilator of deceitful men. A plethora of straight-to-video shockers wallow in medical excess, including the notorious *Guinea Pig* (1985–1990) series of films, which offer dissections of tortured individuals in a grunge-like but clinically disinterested manner. In the 'medical experiment gone awry' *Megyaku: Akuma no yorokobi* (*Naked Blood*, 1995) a drug which causes the brain to associate pain with pleasure results in sickeningly protracted scenes of self-mutilation and even self-cannibalism.

But it's not all hard-gore – these films are in many ways underground productions appealing to a specialist market – and the modern Japanese horror film still has a heavy reliance on a spiritual and literary legacy, predominantly in feeling and aesthetic. Shimizu Takashi's ongoing *Ju-On* (*The Grudge*, 2000) series of films replace narrative coherence with a refined sense of atmosphere and dread. Although his US remake of the film is more overtly gory, the slow-burn menace of the first Japanese cinema release (he had already made it as a TV movie) is hard to shake off. The premise is, like *Ringu*, elegantly simple and plausibly preposterous. A brutal double murder has left a house in Tokyo contaminated with a grudge that curses all who enter it. This is essentially a peg on which to hang a series of tense creeps and scares, often executed with decidedly low-tech but unnerving effects – reversed film making hair spread over the walls, sudden jump cuts, shadows darting across the camera's foreground. In one sequence our heroine is suffering flash-backs in front of the mirror recalling her encounter with a creepy, sheet-white mute boy. Holding her hands to her head, she suddenly realises that there are three hands touching her face, and one of them does not seem to belong to a living being…

Japanese horror encompasses a whole gamut of themes from haunted houses (*Honogurai mizu no soko kara* [*Dark Water*, 2002]), vampires (Yamamoto Michio's *Noroi no yakata: Chi o sû me* [*Lake of Dracula*, 1971]), psychotic families (*Inugamike no ichizoku* [1976, 2006]) and zombie splatter (*Versus*, 2000) along with more traditional-based *kaidan*. It's a market that shows no sign of stopping, even though the heights of *Ring*-mania are probably over, with straight-to-video (V-Cinema) horror booming and the genre being a staple part of the television drama schedule. As with any Japanese genre there are also anime horrors to enjoy, including the ever popular Nagai Gō character *Devilman* (1973 on), *Vampire Princess Miyu* (1988), *Vampire Hunter D* (1983), *Blood: The Last Vampire* (2000), *Hellsing* (2002) and *Witch Hunter Robin* (2002). Japanese horror cinema is probably the most prolific in the world after the US but its product range is far more diverse in its outlook and overall effect.

Hong Kong Horror Cinema

The rich and extensive cultural wealth of China can be daunting – a vast and varied landscape that has embraced myth and modernity with aplomb for thousands of years. At times the blurring between history and mythology exceeds that of the Greek epic writers as interventions from the spiritual planes affect the martial world with often heroic, normally tragic, results. In this heady melange it is hardly surprising that the spirit world is inexorably intertwined with the martial world, that there are demons, magic and ghosts all around. Normally these spiritual creatures are unseen or quiet, but when they are riled, when their shrines are desecrated or abandoned, their malevolent wrath is terrifying to behold. Tales of ghosts, fox spirits (*huli jing* – although the term has overtones of seductress) and demons have permeated Chinese literature for millennia. Perhaps the most influential proponent is Pu Songling, a wandering tutor of modest income who collected, Brothers Grimm style, folk tales during his travels, compiling them in his book *Strange Stories from a Chinese Studio* (1679). The book didn't receive widespread popularity until sometime after his death but its influence on art, theatre, literature and eventually comic books and film were immense. Because of this many Chinese horror films have tended towards period settings with elements of phantasmagoria. Although this trend eventually gave way to contemporary ghost films the literary roots of the genre are still apparent. This commentary here refers mainly to Hong Kong Chinese cinema because mainland horror films were effectively outlawed for much of the twentieth century.

Hong Kong is one of the most densely populated territories in the world, a bustling, vibrant place of commerce. A British colony until 1997 and with its political and economic independence assured until 2046, Hong Kong is in a unique position as a gateway to one of the world's fastest-emerging economies, with a history aligned to a previous global superpower. At its height, the Hong Kong film industry was the third largest in the world (after Hollywood and Bollywood), punching way above its weight considering its population of less than seven million people. Born from the traditions of Chinese literature and Chinese opera/theatre, it is characterised by a lack of regard for Western concepts of realism and highly stylised, emotionally intense content. Theatre troupes provided Hong Kong films with much of their physicality – Chinese opera is breathtakingly acrobatic – while the adoption of traditional texts, fantastical swordplay (*wu xia*) and martial arts embellished the productions. Sadly much of early Hong Kong cinema was destroyed during the Japanese occupation from 1941 to 1945 but the years following the war saw the emergence of a strong film industry, fuelled by an influx of talent from the mainland and buoyed by the marketing potential throughout South East Asia. Hong Kong cinema had become just as much about creating a territorial export cinema as a local one.

Early Chinese horror films tended to centre on ghost or *huli jing* tales of lost loves or tragic romantic entanglements with spirits, such as Beihai Li's now lost *Yanzhi* (1925). Indeed the boundaries between romantic tragedy, love triangle and supernatural horror were often paper-thin in films such as *A Maid's Bitter Story* (1949) and *Ghost Woman of the Old Mansion* (1949) which constituted some of the few spiritual-based pictures made following the war. *Enchanting Shadow* (1958) perfectly blended the corporeal and spiritual worlds to create a film that was at once romantic and scary, emphasising a more overtly horrific angle to its tale of doomed romance. For the next decade or so super-natural elements would be common in many films but not provide the main impetus for the plot.

The 1970s saw the Hong Kong film industry go into hyperdrive, madly floundering to find a successor to the international phenomenon that was Bruce Lee, but also sowing the seeds for a more sustained batch of horror films. *The Legend of the 7 Golden Vampires* (1974) was first out of the stalls, a hybrid of Hammer and Shaw Brothers at a time when both companies were desperate for a hit, relocating Van Helsing to China for equal measures of kung-fu and undead action. It's a lively, energetic, exploitation mess that did little to revive the companies' fortunes. Another set of financial misfires would beset upcoming director Tsui Hark whose first film *The Butterfly Murders* (1979) is a bizarre blend of *wu xia*, whodunnit and horror as a group of disparate fighters come across a deserted castle whose inhabitants have been apparently devoured by savage butterflies, shown in surrealistic gory glory in one of the film's many flashback sequences. Tsui followed his debut with the satirical cannibal film *We're Going to Eat You* (1980), a sort of *Carry On Cannibal Ferox*. Not only did audiences not relate to it, the censors were not amused either. Tsui would continue baiting author-ities and audiences alike until he found himself at the forefront of a new wave of Hollywood-literate filmmakers who reinvented Hong Kong cinema as a flagship of world entertainment.

Perhaps bizarrely, the surge in specifically period horror came from Sammo Hung, the rotund but astonishingly athletic kung-fu artist who had been trained in the same Chinese opera academy as fellow stars Jackie Chan and Yuen Biao. Sammo brought the spirit of Pu Songling to the modern Hong Kong film, something of a box-office risk at the time, in *Encounters of the Spooky Kind* (1980), an almost peerless blend of comedy, horror and kung-fu. The cuckolded and hapless 'Brave' Cheung (Hung) gambles away his limited funds by surviving nights spent alone in haunted properties – in fact, elaborate cons by his so-called friends. However, the fake hauntings attract the wrath of the genuine dead and, before long, Cheung is desperately escaping the gravity-defying clutches of a corpse and pleading with the local police that he is not responsible for a number of local deaths. Hung's ability to look comically uncoordinated yet supremely dextrous is one of the key factors in the film's success through its contradictions – of real versus fake, of horror versus comedy. However, despite the humour, *Encounters of the Spooky Kind* has its fair share of scares, of the maggot-ridden undead and of demonic possession. Possession of another kind, and more overtly referencing Pu Songling, is *The Dead and the Deadly* (1982), by Hung regular Wu Ma, where Hung's character is even more idiotic than he was in *Encounters*. Again infidelity and double crossing are the name of the game but the film really excels when Hung is possessed by the spirit of his dead employer – who for reasons too complicated to go into here was thought to be dead, but wasn't – and slapstick violence ensues.

During this period, Hung was involved in many comedies and kung-fu films but he returned to horror, producing *Mr Vampire* (*Jiangshi Xiansheng*, 1985), the film that launched a hundred imitators. The *jiangshi dianying*[10] or 'cadaver film' would become a staple genre in its own right. Labelled vampire films, these differ from their western counterparts, although the western style of vampire does creep into the narrative of such offshoots as *Doctor Vampire* (1991). *Mr Vampire* goes some way towards establishing the ground rules for the hopping-corpse film, mixing kung-fu and humour along with the scares. Later films would balance things differently, usually becoming more comic but occasionally increasing the gore factor.

Naturally, other companies weren't going to sit by and let Sammo dominate the market. *Human Lanterns* (1982) is a hysterically *Grand Guignol* period piece about a mad lantern-maker who fashions his wares from the flayed flesh of his female victims. Similar 'human fashion' would crop up in films such as *Horrible High Heels* (1996) – no explanation needed for where the shoe leather came from. Meanwhile a young Chow Yun Fat was eking out a living appearing in low-budget horror such as *The Witch from Nepal* (1985) and the truly deranged anthropological corpse god film *The Seventh Curse* (1986). Tsui Hark had been creating a revolution of his own with *Zu: Warriors from the Magic Mountain* (1983), a landmark in Hong Kong film history because of the way it married western-style model and effects techniques with a distinctly Chinese aesthetic, bringing the wirework and fantasy elements of Chinese film culture into a modern and vibrant age. The screen literally sears with ideas and images: ghostly flying women with endless ribbon trails, thousand-eyed monsters, a man saving the martial plane from destruction by holding back a meteor with the strength of his eyebrows. Hark had a protégé in the shape of wirework choreographer Ching Sui-Tung whom he set to work on *A Chinese Ghost Story* (1987), an inventive and romantic mix of ghostly apparitions, tree demons and the seductive dead. This time the film was solidly based upon and indeed credited to Pu Songling's tales. The film's success led to two sequels, both directed by Ching – the final chapter, a breathtakingly strange descent into a Felliniesque disco hell. The films had a number of successful spin-off cash-ins in the *Erotic Ghost Story* (1990) series.

Fox spirits, nymphs and the hopping dead made up the fantasy side of the market, but horror had a grislier niche in the realm of the contemporary film. Often based upon real-life crime many of these were branded as Category III films, a certificate which was designed initially to delineate pornography from mainstream filmmaking but was increasingly used to foster exploitation films. Interestingly, even though a Cat III rating could result in less commercial revenue, it didn't preclude critical acclaim. *The Untold Story* (*Human Pork Buns,* 1993) was a queasy and squalid look into the mind of a xenophobic rapist and murderer who disposes of his victims by cooking them as pork buns, even selling them to the police investigating the disappearances. Anthony Wong deservedly won a best actor award for his truly sleazy but mesmerising performance. It spawned a number of imitators, both in the official sequel and even in such quality productions as Fruit Chan's politicised *Dumplings* (2004).

Cat III shockers have the advantage of low costs and revenues yielded predominantly from the video market. What's surprising is how many of these films made it into cinemas, a situation unlikely to occur in the US or UK. While some films are purely exploitative – a more outrageously tasteless cash-in-on-news-headlines would be harder to imagine than *Ebola Syndrome* (1996) – many have a grim nihilism that is at odds with their lowest-common-denominator concepts. *Dr Lamb* (1993) stars Simon Yam Tat Wah as a cabbie-cum-killer being interrogated by the police force. His misogynist crimes of rape and butchery result in a search of his apartment that unearths various body parts, in a scene deemed too unpleasant for the Hong Kong censors of the time. *Dr Lamb* was directed by Billy Tang Hin Sing, whose assaults on good taste were countered by his ability to elicit excellent performances and production values on low-budget shoots. In many ways, Tang's films are too well made to be dismissed as simple exploitation despite furnishing cinema with some of its more unforgettably unsound moments, notably the immolation of a little girl in front of her father in *Run and Kill* (1993) and the monumentally offensive *Red to Kill* (1994), about a serial killer and necrophile who targets young girls at a mental home.

The 1997 handover of Hong Kong from the British to the Chinese had a profound effect, with the film industry fearing a backlash against the relative freedom of expression they had had under British rule (relative in that Britain was hardly the bastion of cinematic freedoms) and many top talents seeking opportunities elsewhere. But the fears were unfounded as China stuck with the terms of the handover agreement. The concern put a dent in the filmmaking community, however, which then struggled to return to its glory days of the 1980s and early 1990s. But this brief dip in the confidence of the established community did allow a new generation of filmmakers to get a foothold in a market that had become increasingly insular.

Although born and raised in Hong Kong, twin brothers Oxide and Danny Pang initially made their mark in the Thai film industry with a number of thrillers and the portmanteau horror film *Bangkok Haunted* (2001), before returning to Hong Kong to make *The Eye* (2002). The Pang Brothers' work is typified by their sense of extremely stylised aesthetics and attention to colour (indeed Oxide had worked as a film colourist in Hong Kong) coupled with fluid camerawork that is as comfortable dashing around like a beast possessed as quietly, almost imperceptibly, tracking onto some scene of impending horror. *The Eye* is a supreme example of their filmmaking, a slow-burning post-*Ringu* set-up, in which a blind girl is given an eye transplant and begins to see shadows of the dead, with a killer punch-line as simple as it is horrific... followed by a huge-scale set-piece of destruction with mystical revelations and featuring eye-popping (excuse the pun) special effects. It's like having two horror films in one, the creepy and the rollercoaster. Suddenly the brothers became the face of high-quality horror entertainment, delivering sequels *The Eye 2* (2004) and, confusingly, *Eye 10* (2006).

Korean Horror Cinema

Korea is currently enjoying a golden era of cinema, its films and filmmakers becoming increasingly well known on the international stage. However, Korea's history since the invention of cinema has been one of turbulence and occupation and as a result its film industry has been influenced by the politics of the time. Korea was occupied by Japan in the first half of the twentieth century and then, following Japan's defeat in World War Two, divided into two zones. Cold War politics took over and the Communist North invaded the South in 1950, starting the Korean War, which was over within the decade but still remains essentially unresolved. Sadly most of Korea's early films were destroyed during these bloody years. North Korea remains one of the most mysterious and secretive countries on earth and, although it is well known that its president is a film fanatic, little is known of the country's film industry.

The Korean film industry has always been at the mercy of the government and tax breaks were introduced in the 1950s to help boost local production. A new wave of Korean cinema was born, but not without authority interference – for the next few decades the state would have a large say in what could be seen and how many films could be produced. Kim Ki-young made a number of dark, twisted psychological films, mainly focusing on women in a melodramatic context. His most famous work *Hanyo* (*The Housemaid*, 1960) is ostensibly about a married man seduced by his housemaid, and when his wife finds out, the relationship between them all turns into a torrid and disturbing power struggle. Filmed in black and white, this is a powerful examination of psychological horror. The film was released during a brief window of relaxation of Korea's censorship laws and it is unlikely that such a film would have been made even a couple of years later.

A popular sub-genre of the horror film in Korea is that of the ghost story (*kuei-dam*), which gained particular prominence in the late 1960s and throughout the 1970s, generally involving murder victims returning from the dead to wreak revenge upon those who had wronged them. In many ways these were more populalist versions of *Hanyo* but normally blended with ghosts, and occasionally vampires, for example *Ahkea Khots* (1961), a Korean answer to the popular Hammer film *Horror of Dracula*. Despite the country's occasional political fracas with Japan, a large amount of Japanese culture also influenced (and continues to influence) Korean cinema. The *kaiju* (big monster) film was a successful genre with *Yonggary, Monster from the Deep* (1967) emerging as the most enduring of Korean monsters. *Ujugoe-in Wangmagwi* (1967) was also popular. In a bizarre twist, one of the early monster movies was remade as *Pulgasari* in 1985 by prolific filmmaker Shin Sang-ok. Bizarre in that Shin Sang-ok made the film in North Korea having allegedly been kidnapped to make films for producer, and future head of state, Kim Jong-il. Shin Sang-ok had regularly made horror films in South Korea during times when censorship conditions allowed, giving us *Ijo geodam* (*Ghosts of Chosun,* 1970), in which the ghosts of a suicidal woman and her wrongly executed husband join an almost vampiric cat to wreak vengeance on a lecherous noble, *Banhonnyeo* (*Woman with Half a Soul,* 1973), about a man unaware that his wife is a ghost, and *Sanyeo* (*The Snake Woman,* 1969), in which a snake is transformed by a demon into a beautiful woman in order to seduce a Buddhist monk and produce an unholy child.

Government control began to tighten in the 1970s and films started to be used as propaganda tools, which proved to be hugely unpopular with audiences. The whole industry went into a savage decline. After a politically turbulent couple of years from 1979–80, which included a coup d'etat, a presidential assassination and a massacre, South Korea's government slowly began edging back towards democracy. In 1988, foreign films were allowed access to the Korean marketplace. The result at once devastated and paradoxically revitalised the industry – at first it squeezed domestic product out of the market, but then forced it to adapt to survive, which ultimately it did through the imposition of a quota system that obliged cinemas to screen Korean films for a portion of each year. The introduction of film schools saw the emergence of a new generation of talent, unhindered by the need to adhere to the strict censorship of the past.

Many Korean films reflect the desire for reunification and this was borne out in the many tragic, yet graphic, war films produced from the late 1990s onwards. *Shiri* (1999), a *Nikita*-style thriller about a North Korean assassin, then Park Chan-wook's moving *Joint Security Area* (2000) proved that there was an enormous market for home-made product and the Korean blockbuster was born. There was even a war-horror hybrid in the ghostly tale *R-Point* (2004), about a group of soldiers who have to face adversaries both living and dead. *Whispering Corridors* (1998), directed by Park Ki-hyeong, was one of the first of the new wave of Korean horror, so successful that it spawned semi-sequels *Memento Mori* (1999) and *Wishing Stairs* (2003). The success of the Japanese *Ringu* probably had as much impact, even resulting in an official Korean remake, *The Ring Virus* (1999), a more sexualised version of the story, which tries to explain the origins of the cursed tape, than the more ambiguous *Ringu*.

Park Ki-hyeong also made *Acacia* (2003), a visually arresting and disturbing film about an adopted boy whose erratic behaviour and affection for a large acacia tree, which he thinks is the reincarnation of his mother, leads to tragedy. In one scene the entire house is tied up with crimson wool as though bleeding to death but the film's ace card lies in creating horror from what is generally thought of as an inanimate object. But this acacia can kill, its razor-sharp leaves slicing the guilty, their dead eyes staring in terror as ants crawl from beneath their eyelids.

What is interesting about Korean horror is that much of it defies simple classification. Park Chan-wook's celebrated *Vengeance* trilogy contains some of the most extreme scenes of recent years, but can they be defined as horror? *Old Boy* (2003), the second film in the series, most certainly can. A man held in solitary confinement for years by unseen captors seeks his bloody revenge, but the incarceration has left him unable to distinguish between reality and hallucination. With scenes of explicit violence including an extended scene of a claw hammer murder and the eating of a live octopus, the chilling consequences are terrifying and utterly memorable. Far less graphic and bizarre, Ahn Byeong-ki's *Phone* (2002) nevertheless gets under the skin despite its rather ropey premise of a mobile phone whose owners end up texting the choir invisible. Containing spooky renditions of the *Moonlight Sonata*, sudden jumps when glancing at the bathroom mirror, gratuitous rain and, everyone's favourite, the spooky kid, *Phone* has them all and more. As a result of its theme of child abuse and the genuinely powerful acting of Seo-Woo Eun as a child who veers from pleasantries to screaming psychosis in the blink of an eye, it uses all its elements to disturbing effect.

Indian Horror Cinema

'Indian film industry is the largest in the world producing over a thousand films in an year seen over 13000 cinema halls. Every three months an audience as large as India's entire population flock to the cinema halls'[*sic*][11]

In terms of the sheer number of films produced, the Indian film industry is the largest in the world. Although Bollywood – Hindi cinema based in Mumbai – is the best known centre of Indian cinema there are a number of other regions that also contribute to the country's most colourful export, for example Telegu (Tollywood), Tamil (Kollywood), Malayalam, Bengali and Kannada. Indian films are generally characterised by their 'masala' nature, with as many genres as possible rolled into one. They will often contain drama, action, romance, comedy and fisticuffs, all interspersed with a variety of song and dance numbers. This approach is designed to appeal to as wide an audience, and as lucrative a box office, as possible. As such, directors and producers tend not to restrict themselves to a single theme. A slight deviation from this formula occurs when looking at the Indian horror film, a popular but minor part of the country's film output. Generally speaking, the Indian horror film is made outside of Mumbai and treated with some disdain by the wider film and video-watching audience – like many countries, horror is seen as the disreputable cousin to respectable entertainment.

The earliest Indian horror films were ghost stories, supernatural thrillers about reincarnation or rebirth. *Mahal* (1949) is essentially a haunted house story with a complex plot filmed in an expressive style unusual for the time. A young man finds that the house he has inherited is not all it seems and ghostly apparitions haunt the grounds. Despite repeated warnings he is drawn back to the house, intoxicated by the supernatural presence there and convinced he is the reincarnation of one of two doomed lovers. The film's popularity, along with its famous soundtrack (the song *Aayega Aanewala* is one of the best-selling songs of all time) and remakes, have made this a perennial favourite, a tragic romance film that is apparently supernatural.

As with other film industries the Indian censorship regulations placed restraints on what could be shown on screen, so many of the earlier examples of the horror genre tend to be spiritual pieces or tragic dramas with a supernatural element rather than visceral in their content. Similar restrictions on sex and nudity have continued to this day with studios constantly testing the boundaries of what is deemed acceptable to the Central Board of Film Certification, India's film censorship board. However, the influence of Hollywood on Indian filmmakers did have an impact on the thematic content of Indian cinema. The worldwide success of *The Exorcist* was repeated in India and soon demonic possession became a popular theme in locally produced horror films, spawning many remakes, the most famous of which was *Gehrayee* (1980). There are a multitude of Indian folk tales but, because of the Hindu custom that bodies should be cremated, these stories tended to focus on spiritual or possessive horror (hence the popularity of *The Exorcist*) rather than that of reanimation. The vampire and zombie films that are made in India derive from their western counterparts and have little relationship to indigenous myth. Indeed the horror genre as a whole is one that has relied heavily on appropriation and is still viewed disapprovingly by many, not only for visual content but also because of its cultural irrelevance.

Although there were a few genre films starring A-list actors, the horror film in India was dominated by lower-budget productions. The Ramsay Brothers, purveyors of fine B-movie shockers, became enormously popular and pleasingly disreputable. A true family franchise, the Ramsays comprised seven brothers, sons of FU Ramsay, all of whom had specific roles in the filmmaking process: Shyam & Tulsi were responsible for direction, Kumar provided the screenplays, Arjun was involved with production design or associate direction, Gangu was the cinematographer, Kiran the soundman and Keshu brought the whole lot together as producer. Their films were characterised by their low production values and ensemble casts, but despite their B-movie roots, the films were entertaining and hugely popular. Their themes again revolved around the supernatural – evil spirits and monster movies – and in the Bollywood tradition included song and dance numbers as well as comic interludes. They also pushed the boundaries, including as much sex and nudity as India's notoriously conservative censor would allow, often finding themselves at loggerheads with the authorities not only for the films themselves but the suggestive publicity material surrounding them. Their most successful film was *Purana Mandir* (1984), so popular that it instantly spawned a sequel, *Saamri* (1985). Other major films from the prolific family included *Haveli* (1985), *Veerana* (1985), *Tahkhana* (1986), *Dak Bangla* (1987), *Purani Haveli* (1989) and *Bandh Darwaza* (1990).

Naturally other filmmakers were eager to follow the Ramsay Brothers' successes. Unable to compete with even the Ramsays' production values, writer/producer/director Mohan Bhakri made up for his budget limitations by filling his films with copious quantities of sex and violence, resulting in high-exploitation shockers such as the revenge thriller *Cheekh* (1985). Always eager to research Hollywood trends by noting key elements in popular franchises, Bhakri had his biggest hit with the luridly enjoyable monster movie *Khooni Mahal* (1987), surprising many in the industry.

Ram Gopal Varma is one of Bollywood's most respected directors whose trademark is innovation in an industry that doesn't tend to deviate from popular narratives and styles. Varma's first foray into the horror genre was *Raat* (1992), a supernatural thriller about a house that may or may not be haunted. As he developed his reputation he started working in the gangster genre. *Satya* (1998) was violent and brutal and shot in a documentary style, which coined the term 'Mumbai-noir'. Known for his willingness to throw convention to the wind he made *Bhoot* (2003), an almost revolutionary film because it didn't contain musical numbers or comedy. Genuinely scary – *bhoot* is Hindi for ghost – it confounded the industry by becoming a box-office hit. Varma was also one of the directors of the portmanteau horror piece *Darna Zaroori Hai* (2006).

Vikram Bhatt, the director of modestly budgeted but imaginatively shot films for his family's business, has garnered a reputation as a maker of scary thrillers mixed with popular songs often directly inspired by Hollywood counterparts: *Kasoor* (2001), for example, was derived from *Jagged Edge* (1985). *RaaZ* (2002), a reworking of *What Lies Beneath* (2000), sees a couple trying to patch up their marriage by revisiting the house in which they fell in love, a house that now seems to be haunted by a malevolent spirit. Its success spawned a new wave of supernatural thrillers. In *Saaya* (2003) a doctor's wife dies tragically, but her soul returns from the dead to find her lover. Everyone around the doctor thinks he's going insane with grief and refuses to listen to his protestations of spiritual visitations. *Hawa* (2003) made full use of its special effects budget to create a haunted house story where a modern woman and her family fall prey to an evil force of damned souls. Again the emphasis is on the victims whose stories of supernatural encounters aren't believed, a matter made more disturbing and relevant by the film's theme of sexual assault, a subject that can only be seriously broached in a film about supernatural entities without fear of heavy censorship. *Darna Mana Hai* (2003) is a portmanteau piece with six stories interwoven to form an overall arc as a group of friends tell each other spooky tales after their car inconveniently breaks down. As the creepy stories are relayed, Amicus style, the tellers begin to go missing in equally spooky circumstances.

Although horror does not seem to have found a true niche in mainstream Indian cinema, a number of scary movies do crop up from year to year and, in tune with much of the rest of the world, are currently very popular, particularly amongst the young. Gone though are the ghosts of old and the Ramsays' monsters. Modern Indian horror has been brought bang up to date. Partly this is through western influences but also due to some relaxations by the Central Board of Film Certification which, while still forbidding explicit nudity, is now more open to scenes of terror, preferring to concentrate on politically sensitive films rather than entertainment. That said, the guidelines still state that 'pointless or avoidable scenes of violence, cruelty and horror, scenes of violence primarily intended to provide entertainment and such scenes as may have the effect of de-sensitising or de-humanising people are not shown'[12].

Gojira (Godzilla) (1954), Japan

Directed by: Honda Ishiro
Starring: Takarada Akira, Kôchi Momoko, Hirata Akihiko, Shimura Takashi

Gojira has a reputation based upon a series of enjoyable but camp psychedelic cheapies notable for their cheesy dubbing in western prints. However the difference between this view and the original film could not be more pronounced. *Gojira* argues against the proliferation of nuclear arms and the testing of nuclear weapons (never explicitly aimed at America but the film opens with a nuclear test destroying a Japanese fishing boat in an incident mirroring one that occurred off Bikini Atoll). With its tacit criticism of the arms race, when the film finally reached US shores all references to a nuclear reason for the rise of the beast were excised and Raymond Burr added to fill in the gaps, reducing the film to a conventional monster movie.

The plot is *kaiju* simplicity – an atomic test awakens a beast from the depths of the ocean and it devastates Japan. The only person who has the means to destroy the beast, Serizawa-sensei, faces a moral dilemma as he wishes to end the destruction but does not want another lethal weapon to be known to the world. What is so striking about *Gojira* is the sheer scale of the attacks. Trains are wrenched from their tracks, pylons mangled and huge urban areas are reduced to rubble and ashes. The child of the atom bomb produces devastation not just through his crushing reptilian feet but in his toxic radioactive breath. *Gojira* was a prestige movie for the time, costing ten times that of a normal production, but even so the scale of effects work meant that the filmmakers could not afford to produce the beast through stop-frame animation. Instead *Gojira* is an impressively filmed man in a suit demolishing perfectly miniaturised sets, optically composited with live action. The results are astonishing as whole cities are razed thanks to the pioneering work of Tsuburaya Eiji, Japan's foremost effects technician. The balance between the terror of the destruction and entertaining spectacle is one of the tightropes that a great disaster movie must tread and *Gojira* succeeds at every turn. An anti-war environmental film replete with spectacular apocalyptic destruction and a giant, iconic, radioactive lizard. Beware inferior imitations.

The mighty *Gojira* unleashes radioactive destruction on Japan.

Enchanting Shadow (1958), Hong Kong

Directed by: Li Han Hsiang
Starring: Lei Zhao, Betty Loh Ti

When there's no room at the inn, Ning decides to stay in a decrepit and remote temple, despite warnings that it is haunted. At night he is lured by the sound of music to a part of the temple seemingly untouched by decay and spies the beautiful Hsiao Chen, with whom he soon forms a relationship, helping her finish delicate poems with the swish of a calligrapher's brush. But is Hsiao Chen who she seems and why is she so afraid of her cantankerous grandmother?

Li Han Hsiang would become famous for a series of elegant and lavish musicals, qualities that mark *Enchanting Shadow* with a sense of poetic lyricism; the repetition of the poem as a leitmotif, the repeated shots of Hsiao Chen framed by the hole in Ning's crumbling bedroom wall, the contrast of the temple by night and day, of the old and new, the dead and the living. Rather than turn the film into a spiritual melodrama this accentuates the feeling of morbid dread set against a backdrop of doomed love. Stylistically *Enchanting Shadow* excels in its use of studio-bound but elaborate sets, which allow for evocative and elaborate lighting effects. Hsiao Chen's tragic ghost is indicated as much through gesture, composition and tears as through dialogue, and she's often dissected by light and shadow. When the horrible truth is finally revealed, the film becomes genuinely horrific with decomposing vampire demons shedding blood as crimson and glowing as any Hammer horror.

The title is as elegant, succinct and descriptive as the film itself, a seductive tragedy as morbid as it is moving. Based upon the story by Pu Songling, *Enchanted Shadow* would get a glossy, effects-laden, saucy remake in the form of *A Chinese Ghost Story*.

Jigoku (Hell) (1960), Japan

Directed by: Nakagawa Nobuo
Starring: Amachi Shigeru, Numata Yoichi, Mitsuya Utako

Although he made nearly 100 films, the reputation of Nakagawa Nobuo lies with a small series of horror movies, including *Ghost of Yotsuya* (1959), a red-blooded take on the genre with influential and disorientating effects work. *Jigoku* is one of the most daringly original and visually arresting made in this period, and quite unlike any other. The hero Shiro is mirrored by the conscience-free Tamura, his alter ego. After Tamura accidentally kills a drunken yakuza and flees the scene things start going drastically wrong for Shiro, resulting in numerous bizarre deaths and murder attempts. Shiro, dies and, for his sins, goes to Hell. Legally Shiro has done little wrong but *Jigoku* is a film about spiritual hell, of inactivity leading to damnation, where shirking responsibilities is as sinful as actively doing wrong. Over a third of the running time depicts this journey. Although ostensibly similar to Dante's *Inferno*, *Jigoku* takes its visions of Hell from Buddhist temple paintings. Shiro is fervently chasing his unborn daughter, drifting on milky-white rivers or waters of blood, observing the horrors around him. Eyes are gouged out of their sockets, hundreds of dehydrated people crawl desperately to a single waterhole that evaporates in front of them, demons crush sinners with spiked clubs, bodies are ripped asunder and one man is flayed alive, his mouth screaming as his exposed organs pulsate agonisingly for all eternity. Originally intended to be 'Heaven and Hell', somewhere in the pre-production process half the concept was dropped. *Jigoku* is a colourful and horrifying descent into a literally realised spiritual Hell, a nightmarish vision unmatched in the horror genre save in the tortured minds of José Marins or Clive Barker. A truly astonishing and original film.

Onibaba (1964), Japan

Directed by: Shindo Kaneto
Starring: Otowa Nobuko, Yoshimura Jitsuko, Sato Kei

'Demons and snakes may live here'

A cruel but elegant story of sexual desire and murderous survival, *Onibaba* is unflattering in its portrayal of Japanese society during a period of civil war. Two peasant women await the return of their man, respectively son and husband, surviving by selling weapons and armour stolen from dying soldiers, whose bodies they then hurl into a deep hole.

Deadly passions and demonic forces collide in Shindo Kaneto's smouldering *Onibaba*. Toho Company / Photofest © Toho Company

When their loved one's companion Hachi returns, he tells them their wait is futile. The pent-up passions between all three become uncontrollable and the older woman tries to prevent her daughter-in-law eloping with the deserting soldier.

Onibaba hides its rancour and madness in the swaying grasses that cover the landscape. This is society regressing into savagery and primitive instincts seen through a few eyes lurking in the dense undergrowth. The film opens with the two women meticulously and unflinchingly stripping the corpses of two soldiers, dumping their bodies unceremoniously in the gaping vaginal hole that serves as a metaphor for sexual desire, death and decay. The whole sequence is accompanied by the sound of crows awaiting their meal of dead flesh and the rustling, clicking sound of the wind in the grass and bamboo. Throughout, fast tracking shots enhance the urgency of the pair's killing or the younger girl's lust for Hachi. There are no moral scruples here. The older woman realises that if she loses her daughter-in-law to Hachi she is as good as dead but hatches a plan when a samurai sporting an imposing *oni* (demon) mask, falls into her trap. The film's final moments are pure gothic horror as the true curse of the *oni* mask becomes apparent.

At turns bleak and morbid, yet unbridled in its passion, the presence of the demonic mask adds a further macabre dimension to this tale of madness, claustrophobia and human depravity. *Onibaba* is as much a film about metaphorical *oni* as literal ones.

Yabu no naka no kuroneko (Black Cat) (1968), Japan

Directed by: Shindo Kaneto
Starring: Sato Kei, Taichi Kiwako, Otowa Nobuko, Nakamura Kichiemon

A mother, Yone, and her daughter-in-law, Shige, await the return of their brave samurai Gintoki, but, unlike in *Onibaba,* it is not they who survive the factional fighting. A group of passing soldiers rape and kill the pair, their bloodied bodies lying spreadeagled among the charred ruins of their house. But they are revived, at least at night, by a black cat, a *bakeneko*, lapping at their faces. The two seek revenge by seducing passing samurai, playing with and finally killing their prey, ripping their throats out with gleeful enthusiasm. But one of their potential victims is Gintoki, returned from the wars and the pair now find themselves facing a dilemma.

Shindo fills his frame with dreamy eroticism and ethereal promise; despite being made in the late 1960s, the film is shot in black and white for aesthetic reasons, enhancing the otherworldly nature of the proceedings. Unlike *Onibaba*'s down-to-earth peasant lust and regression, *Kuroneko* is as sleek and seductive as its feline title suggests – like a cat it is sensuous but deadly and remorseless. *Kuroneko* has all the pacing and visual elements of a dream, natural yet unreal. The misty bamboo forest cuts imposing angles across the scene, the daughter always jumps delicately in slow-motion over puddles as though averse to water, while the spirits glide over the mounted samurai foretelling their imminent doom. Savagery, suicide and surrealism combine to drive the film to its inevitably tragic finale. Choreographed to perfection, *Kuroneko*'s complex yet elegant tale is part elegiac ghost story, part tragedy and part examination of class commitments in a time of social upheaval. At turns breathtaking, poetic and horrific, the blend of eroticism and brutality is an intoxicating mix.

Inugamike no ichizoku (The Inugami Family) (1976), Japan

Directed by: Ichikawa Kon
Starring: Ishizaka Koji, Takamine Mieko, Aoi Teruhiko

Yokomizo Seishi found fame writing macabre tales of murder and historical ghost stories, spurred on initially by the father of Japanese weird detective fiction, Edogawa Rampo. *The Inugami Family* is a gothic story of hate, incest, greed and violence, part melodrama, part giallo, the name Inugami recalling loyal dog spirits of Japanese folklore, often used to exact vengeance. When the wealthy polygamous elder Inugami dies, his will stipulates that his entire estate will be inherited by family outsider Tamayo, providing she marries one of his three sons, each born from a different wife. Naturally the news is not welcomed and before long a series of brutal murders occurs, narrowing Tamayo's matrimonial choices, should she decide to marry.

Ichikawa's first take on this often-filmed tale (he remade it himself 30 years later) exudes mistrust through its inventive use of freeze frames, old photo inserts and jump cuts to disorientate the viewer and leave them as paranoid as the characters. This is a film about families, betrayal and ritual, of maintaining a veil of respectability whilst plotting schemes that would make Lady Macbeth blanch. Although the mothers are seen as the manipulators behind the scenes, each trying to oust the others' boys from the equation, it is the third son Sukekiyo (or is he...?) who strikes the imagination. Having been hideously scarred in the war his face resembles charred meat on a skull, his eyes staring soullessly from behind the fleshy white rubber mask he uses to disguise his injuries. He's a formidable and eerie figure. Even more strange are the murders themselves, ritualistically based upon the three symbols of the relevant houses: chrysanthemum, koto and axe. When the first son is found murdered, his severed head replaces that of a chrysanthemum-clothed statue. It's a long time before the body is discovered and, in a moment that is pure Poe, his headless corpse, now bloated with gas, rises, legs akimbo, from the bottom of the lake. It's a surreal and macabre moment that typifies this fascinating film, a bloody, intricate and shocking tale of an abusive power whose impact is felt long after death.

Purana Mandir (1984), India

Directed by: Shyam and Tulsi Ramsay
Starring: Mohnish Bahl, Arti Gupta

Purana Mandir is a perfect example of the Ramsay Brothers' approach to low-budget filmmaking – put everything you've got onto the screen and give the audience what they want. Two hundred years ago in Bijapur, the demonic sorcerer Saamri caused havoc – defiling women, drinking the blood of children and desecrating graves. In order to stop his bloody reign this chained fiend was decapitated, his body buried and his head guarded with Shiva's trident. At his semi-execution, Saamri decrees that all of Singh's female heirs will die horribly in childbirth. Fastforward to the present day and the last heir is worried that his daughter, Suman, will also suffer the curse. But she is too busy with her college friends to listen and takes off with boyfriend Sanjay and pals for a jolly in the countryside. There they learn that modernity isn't everything and that demons can rise from their graves to terrorise the living.

Purana Mandir contrasts the city life of discos and permissiveness with the landscape and customs of rural India. This gives the Ramsays plenty of opportunity to show their young starlets in fashionably revealing dress while bemoaning the loss of tradition. Although the opening is suitably operatic, the following hour establishes the social and relational basis of the film, along with a variety of songs and some martial arts, romance and humour. When it becomes clear that all is not well in the countryside the film moves into overdrive using every trick in the book to spook the audience. A simple shower turns into a bloodbath as evil spirits prowl the house. Paintings bleed when stabbed. Lightning forks emphasise the evil powers at work. The local villagers try to appease the reawakened Saamri with the sacrifice of the youngsters. It all moves at such a pace, the two-and-a-half hour running time shoots by in a blur of whip shots and zooms, Dutch tilts, spooky groans, animal noises, fog, singing and violence. Bloody, sexy and fun, the film proved so popular that the brothers ploughed on to make a semi-sequel *Purana Mandir 2: Saamri* (1985), which further enhanced the viewing experience by being shot in 3-D.

Mr Vampire (1985), **Hong Kong**

Directed by: Lau Kun Wai
Starring: Lam Ching Ying, Moon Lee

A landmark in Hong Kong cinema, *Mr Vampire* launched a seemingly endless stream of *jiangshi dianying* sequels and imitators while revitalising the career of its star Lam Ching Ying, forever linking the actor with his dynamic Van Helsing-style character. Kau and his two hapless assistants have to mind the mortuary business while their boss is out strolling with corpses in the countryside. In three days they need to re-bury Mr Yam because a botched interment has resulted in bad *feng shui*, but the corpse bursts free and rampages across the countryside. *Mr Vampire* is a near-flawless blend of comedy, horror, effects work and action. The manic opening, in which Kau's bumbling assistants see a practical joke culminate in the reanimation of eight corpses, is knockabout comedy at its best as the group frantically attempt to halt the dead by slapping prayers on their foreheads.

This black humour mixed with exhilarating acrobatics runs through the film but never detracts from the horror of the vampires or the very real threat they place on the community. There is a bewildering array of myths, customs and weapons used in controlling the living dead and *Mr Vampire* goes to some lengths to establish these in its narrative. Chicken-blood-soaked twine binds a corpse in its coffin, glowing in magical power until a flaw causes the irate undead to explode from its prison and seek retribution. In order to attack the living, the corpse must detect life, so holding your breath is a short-term solution to avoiding unwanted undead attention. The perennial favourite of the genre, sticky rice, can be sprinkled liberally around to dissuade the casual hopping corpse from coming any closer – the effect is like burning coals to the bare-footed dead. The only problem with sticky rice is that it is more expensive than the regular variety so inevitably some unscrupulous merchant will cut the goods to maximise profit, with catastrophic and hilarious results.

Mr Vampire is crammed to the gills with these inventive methods of life-after-death control because it's so eager to fill its running time with as many aspects of the ghost story as possible, even finding time to have one assistant slowly becoming a vampire being bitten and the other falling for the charms of a *huli jing*, succumbing to the world of the dead after an exhaustive night of passion. With evocative lighting, a catchy main song, blood, kung-fu, slapstick and rotted corpses, what more could you ask for?

Rouge (1986), Hong Kong

Directed by: Stanley Kwan
Starring: Anita Mui, Leslie Cheung

Fleur, a 'Flower House' courtesan, is in love with 12th Master Chan but their romance is forbidden on anything other than the level of business transaction. The star-crossed lovers plan an opium-induced suicide so that they can be together for eternity in the netherworld. For over 50 years Fleur walks the roads of Hell alone before returning to the corporeal world to determine the fate of her lover. With the aid of a young couple she seeks the whereabouts of 12th Master.

Fleur cuts a tragically elegant figure from a time where etiquette was everything, and her hosts in the modern city are conspicuously bland in contrast. Kwan uses his film to show Fleur as a subtly real ghost far removed from the demons that typify Hong Kong fantasy cinema. Her appearances and disappearances are disturbingly supernatural but simple – there are no theatrics, she just appears. The real tragedy is that the modern age, for all its advantages, is incapable of true emotional commitment unlike that which Fleur willingly gives to 12th Master. Even though her contemporary friends are in love, the mundanity of modern existence has reduced their passion to one of mutual acceptance – they cannot imagine dying for their love or suffering the eternity of Hell for the other.

Delicate and fleeting, *Rouge* affects on an emotional and spiritual level beyond the visceral and into the existential. Stanley Kwan's exquisite ghost story is unlike any other – quiet, delicate and sophisticated. A lament for a more elegant past but not one without its own exacting cruelties, *Rouge* is a film about roaring passion in a world that has no use for such doomed romanticism. This tragedy is given added poignancy by the early deaths of the film's stars, Leslie Cheung and Anita Mui, who brought the fated lovers so memorably to life.

Shiryo no wana (Evil Dead Trap) (1988), Japan

Directed by: Ikeda Toshiharu
Starring: Ono Miyuki, Katsuragi Aya

'Killing is great fun. But killing by torture is even better.'

Nami, the host of a warped version of *You've Been Framed*, is intrigued by a viewer's videotape sent to her that shows the graphic torture and killing of a young woman. Pulling together her production crew she sets out to investigate the tape's origins at a disused airbase, which is suspiciously easy to break into. Very soon they realise they are out of their depth and being killed off one by one in very deliberate and elaborate ways by a raincoated figure with an unknown grudge.

Evil Dead Trap is a film gloriously out of its time, old fashioned yet surprisingly forward looking. The boom years of the Italian splatter film and giallo may have long passed, but Ikeda and writer Ishii Takashi seem to want to make a Japanese revival of the genre with all dials turned to 11 – even the music sounds like Goblin. Like Ishii's controversial manga (and later as a director himself), *Evil Dead Trap* seems unconcerned with concepts of taste or decency and throws genre convention out of the window in its garish cocktail of sex and violence. The murders are as elaborate as any Argento film – in one scene a perfectly balanced piece of misdirection sees the audience think that a character entering a room will launch a crossbow bolt into the eye of a trussed-up colleague, only for the helpless victim to have half of the front of her face macheted off instead. High-contrast, black-and-white, point-of-view shots, Dutch tilts and jump cuts all go into this stylish, marvellous and gruesomely irresponsible film. Two enjoyably grotesque but inferior sequels followed.

Troublesome Night (1997), Hong Kong

Directed by: Yau Lai-To

'On Ching Ming Festival, it's said that the gate of hell will be opened.'

Occasionally rough around the edges, the low-budget portmanteau film *Troublesome Night* is interesting on a number of levels: as a youth morality picture, an exercise in interlinking narratives and as one of the most rapidly expanding horror franchises – it has spawned 18 sequels and counting. Our host is the sinister moraliser Peter Butt ('usually people call me Peter Prat'), a bizarre guide in that he is both audience confidant but also features in the stories in various guises. He warns of the danger facing the young who disrespect their ancestors, especially on the day of the Ching Ming Festival, the traditional night for the dead that proves the focus for many Chinese horror films. In the first story a group of actors are camping near an ancient graveyard when a trio of possibly ghostly vixens join their nighttime games. Further stories involve an adulterous husband trying to reach a wedding anniversary appointment, a girl whose decision to wear red underwear results in a passionate affair with an invisible demon lover, and finally a haunted cinema with reserved seats 'for local (i.e. dead) people' causing serious problems for a narcissistic actor and his girlfriend.

Troublesome Night's strange blend of overly familiar spook tales is enhanced by its unusual approach to tying four apparently disassociated stories into one interconnected world. For example, the actors in the first story are working on the film made in the second story that is shown projected in the fourth. Memorable scenes include walls bleeding over posters of Tom Cruise, a David Lynch-style neverending corridor of curtains and a football kicked under a toilet cubicle door that becomes a severed head (in a nod, excuse the pun, to Polanski's *The Tenant*). Director Yau Lai-To had previously made the far less moralistic films *The Untold Story* and *Ebola Syndrome*.

Nang-Nak (1998), Thailand

Directed by: Nonzee Nimibutr
Starring: Intira Jaroenpura, Winai Kraibutr

Nonzee Nimibutr has been one of the figures instrumental in the rise of modern Thai cinema both as a producer and a director. *Nang-Nak*, his second film, is a delicate, timeless and spiritual piece interspersed with scenes of graphic supernatural violence. Based upon a Thai legend, the story centres on a young married couple Mak and Nak. Mak is forced to leave his pregnant wife, conscripted into a bloody and brutal war that leaves him physically and mentally scarred. He returns home to enjoy a simple rural existence but an idyllic family life is curtailed when he discovers, but refuses to believe, that his wife died in labour and his child was stillborn. He now resides with the corporeal ghosts of his loved ones, a situation that the local villagers cannot tolerate.

Nang-Nak has it all. Sumptuous but naturalistic photography. Aching love. Savage and brutal revenge. Large-scale war. Small-scale family drama. All the trappings of a vengeful ghost tale are present too: ominous portents of doom signalled by a large spider beating out unnatural rhythms inside Nak's hut, hallucinations of Mak's dead comrade Prig decomposing in his arms, misty ceremonies by the light of the moon. The film's use of unspoilt rural Thailand as a setting means it has a fableistic quality (it has been filmed many times before and since) but one that also has a complex spiritual element. What makes *Nang-Nak* so heartbreaking is that it is in essence the story of people so in love that even death should not part them. Nak's condition is unnatural to the harmony of life and her revenge is motivated purely by a need to be with the man she loves. By turns elegantly simple and spiritually complex, *Nang-Nak* is a tear-jerking combination of supernatural horror and family drama. It went on, deservedly, to become one of the highest-grossing films in Thailand's history.

Ringu (The Ring) (1998), Japan

Directed by: Nakata Hideo
Starring: Matsushima Nanako, Nakatani Miki, Sanada Hiruyuki

Have you seen that strange video, you know, the one everyone's talking about? After you see it you get a phone call and a week later... you die. Reporter Asakawa's seen it. She's investigating the simultaneous deaths of four teenagers, all found with their faces contorted in abject terror. It's an investigation that will lead her, her ex-husband and her son to the brink of death, madness and despair as she pursues the origins of the cursed tape and the awful secret of disturbed teenager Sadako.

Ringu is a prime example of a film that creates its own mythology unburdened by genre convention, creating one of the most disturbing and scary horror films of recent years despite the almost total lack of viscera. Sadako herself is a frightening apparition because even when she is finally revealed to the audience she is still, for the most part, hidden from view, her long matted hair shielding most of her face as she lurches inhumanly towards her next victim. This makes her psychologically far more disturbing, visible yet hidden save for the occasional glimpse of her horrible, bloodshot, evil eye.

Nakata makes full use of his low budget by concentrating on atmospherics and build-up, creating a contemporary myth by updating a standard ghost story with modern technology, although the video itself is grainy, half-seen and deliberately low quality. It is the relentless nihilism, the lack of explanation and the lingering dread that make *Ringu* such an arresting experience. There is no humour, nothing is extraneous and even survival does not provide a happy ending in Sadako's world of madness and misery.

Yeogo kueidam (Whispering Corridors) (1998), Korea

Directed by: Park Ki-hyeong

Closed environments are ideal for the horror film as they offer the protagonists fewer forms of escape, either because of physical or social pressures. Schools provide a perfect horror environment – you have to go there, it's meant to be for your good but is often a source of anguish and misery, which can only be multiplied by the application of a psychotic killer and/or a demonic curse. *Whispering Corridors* follows in this tradition although, as its title suggests, the tone of the film is more melancholic and sinister than bombastic. Importantly, the school itself, supernatural hauntings or unexplained deaths aside, is not a safe environment for its pupils. The teachers are often violent, ruthlessly pursuing the goal of perfect grades to raise the school's, and their own, reputations. The film opens with the hanging of a teacher… but is it suicide? When an ex-pupil returns to the school as a replacement tutor she tries to act as confidante to the frightened girls, particularly So-young, a troubled teenager. Another teacher is found dead in suspicious circumstances and it becomes clear that the past has as much relevance as the present on the state of the school and its well-being.

Park Ki-hyeong's feature debut is less concerned with a body count and more with relationships and the way that the institutionalised environment affects them. *Whispering Corridors* leaves little doubt that this is a supernatural thriller, albeit one played predominantly at a murmur. The sense of unease and menace is profound. When the film's brief sequences of overt supernatural activity play out they are strangely beautiful and ethereal, even in their bloodiness, and are generally realised using in-camera effects (simple jump cuts, careful editing) that make them feel eerily organic. *Whispering Corridors* proved to be a sizeable hit on release and spawned further 'sequels', which tap into a more emotional vein of school horror.

Bhoot (2003), India

Directed by: Ram Gopal Varma
Starring: Ajay Devgan, Urmila Matondkar

'This film of mine is just an attempt to scare you,' consoles director Varma at the opening of *Bhoot*... which he then does. Vishal and Swati's new apartment is an ideal residence for the upwardly mobile couple. Unfortunately the previous tenant Manjeet threw herself and her son to their deaths from the balcony and her restless spirit seems to haunt the building and eventually possess Swati. The film's central premise, a melding of *Ju-On* and *The Exorcist*, is a peg on which Varma hangs a multitude of tricks and scares in the manner of a ghost-train ride. Tortured black figures suddenly appear in mirrors only to vanish again, visions of the past jump into view while quiet, desperate moans fill the corridors and lift-shafts of the apartment block. As Manjeet's spirit begins to take hold of Swati even the apartment cannot contain the hauntings; a pleasant beachside stroll turns into an unexpected scene of phantasmagorical visitation. Vishal wishes to be rational but Swati's continued deterioration forces him to consider a more esoteric solution, and he hires a witch doctor. Even the editing reinforces the idea that the witch doctor possesses powers beyond our understanding; she persuades Manjeet's mother to be present at the exorcism through a series of dissolves rather than via the usual shot-countershot technique. In the film's most elegant chill, Manjeet's son, charred and miserable, stands forlorn on the stairs as the witch doctor glides past him, causing his incorporeal form simply to vanish.

Bhoot's tight cast and claustrophobic settings make for an ideal scare movie as sudden jumps are always accompanied by loud musical flourishes to emphasise the on-screen action. Despite the internal debate about faith and science *Bhoot*'s sole intention is to entertain which, through inventive use of editing and sound, it achieves admirably.

Janghwa Hongryeon (A Tale of Two Sisters) (2003), Korea

Directed by: Kim Ji-woon
Starring: Kim Kap-su, Yum Jung-ah, Lim Su-jeong, Mun Geun-yeong

'What happened that day?'

Kim Ji-woon's insular supernatural horror is a sobering piece about betrayal, hatred, madness and impotence filmed with an innate sense of horrific timing. Returning from an extended stay in a psychiatric institution, sisters Su-Mi and Su-Yeon can only find solace in each other. Their father is vacant and distant while their stepmother, despite showing outward attempts at sympathy, chides them about their dead mother when their father isn't present. Su-Yeon keeps hearing scuttling noises and is visited by horrifying dead figures but could it be that she hasn't recovered fully? Is there really a charred corpse living under the kitchen sink? And what did happen that day?

A Tale of Two Sisters mines the air of family unease to full effect creating a sense of foetid claustrophobia. Largely this is about the escalation of cruelties inflicted by the sisters and the stepmother, but set against a backdrop of supernatural malevolence. Kim Ji-woon times these scenes with ruthless precision – half-seen bodies, the sudden appearance of a woman in green and a horrific, crawling figure under the kitchen sink. The pace is menacing and low-key so that when the shocks do come they really hit home. A film that relies on psychological disquiet in plot and execution, it also embraces visceral horror and surrealism. When a bloodied bag is dragged across the wooden floorboards creating a crimson trail, a terrified Su-Mi tentatively follows its route, her bare feet pattering on the sticky path, as she discovers the horrifying truth.

Brooding, menacing and shocking, the slow-burning gothic tragedy of *A Tale of Two Sisters* leaves a lingering impression of despair and madness.

Saam gaang yi (Three Extremes) (2004), Japan, Hong Kong, Korea

Directed by: Miike Takashi, Fruit Chan, Park Chan-Wook

Anthology films with big name directors tend to be hit-and-miss affairs. *Three Extremes* bucks the trend by presenting three fundamentally different 'extremes' that represent a flavour of contemporary South East Asian cinema.

Director Miike Takashi is not generally renowned for his subtlety but, surprisingly, has very little on his lengthy CV that could be deemed pure horror, although *Audition* and *Masters of Horror: Imprint* (2006) certainly fit the bill. *Box* is unnerving in its quiet, at times totally silent, slice of perfectly composed Japanese gothic. A tortured writer is haunted by nightmares where she is buried in a box by her father, a deed brought on because, in a spate of sibling jealousy, she had accidentally caused her sister's horrific death while rehearsing a contortionist illusionist circus act. Miike shows us horror by implication: the screams of a child being slowly burned alive in an impossibly small box, a single bloodied eye or a half glimpsed shadow skulking away. Individual elements mark out the screen like delicate woodcarvings, the overall effect one of brooding terror.

Dumplings is a stylish, contemporary reworking of the Elizabeth Bathory story by way of Hong Kong exploitation classics like *Human Pork Buns* (1993). A rich housewife seeks out the dingy flat of a specialist dumpling maker, whose delicacies, slightly crunchy to the bite, will give her eternal youth. But the dumplings' special ingredient is procured from maternity clinics in China and smuggled into Hong Kong. The premise alone is enough to put *Dumplings* high on the offensive register but Fruit Chan goes on to show the extent to which sellers and buyers are willing to go, and the horrific consequences of their actions. The viewer's sense of nausea is generated when someone is shown eating normal dumplings, letting their imagination consider the ingredients.

Most operatic of the three is Park Chan-Wook's *Cut*, which features dizzying camerawork and audacious use of sound and editing. As opposed to *Box*, *Cut* revels in its soundtrack to emphasise the dark tale of a film director under siege. The art direction itself is simply stunning as the director's bound and gagged wife is strung up like a puppet at her piano, fingers super-glued to the keys. If her husband does not strangle a child randomly brought off of the streets then she will have her fingers severed one-by-one by a disgruntled extra who has trapped them. The extra's only gripe seems to be that the director is a reasonable man and therefore it isn't fair that he should be rich *and* go to heaven. The combination of the dilemma contrasted with the extravagant use of camera technique make for a compelling and disorientating slice of *Grand Guignol* melodrama.

All *Three Extremes* are perfectly formed mini-dramas (*Dumplings* was expanded to feature length) that are equally unpleasant and adept but stylistically very different.

The Host (2006), Korea

Directed by: Bong Joon-Ho
Starring: Song Kang-ho, Byeon Hie-bong, Park Hae-il, Bae Du-na, Ko Ah-sung

A mortuary worker is ordered by his American boss to dump highly toxic chemicals down the drain, polluting the Han river. Before you can say 'mutant monster' a mutant monster is on the loose, terrorising everyone as it rampages through downtown Seoul. Many are killed in its wake including, apparently, plucky schoolgirl Hyun-Seo. But when her narcoleptic father receives a crackly mobile call whilst in state-imposed quarantine he knows she is still alive. He must become a fugitive in a city disintegrating into panic about viral contagion and find Hyun-Seo.

The Host takes a comforting back-to-basics approach to the monster film but executes it in a way that is relevant to modern concerns. The beast mutated by toxic chemicals harks back half a century but *The Host* takes this B-Movie cliché and runs with it, using the resultant creature – a huge mutant fish with squid-like mouth and the ability to swing like a trapeze artist with its tenticular tail – as a catalyst for concerns about globalisation and state control, as well as preying on fears of recent viral outbreaks such as SARS and avian flu. Up against these incredible odds is an eccentric family simply seeking the truth about the disappearance of their youngest member, taking the film into the realm of family drama. But *The Host* also revels in its great crowd-pleasing set pieces including the elaborate early rampage sequence which sees the beast lashing out at passers-by, tossing them like rag-dolls and swallowing them whole to take back to its lair. The beast itself is a lovingly crafted blend of prosthetic and CGI work and could easily appeal to the same audience as *Jurassic Park* (1993) or the (more gory) *Alligator* (1980). Fully rounded entertainment with heart and a political element that similarly recalls the roots of the monster and *kaiju* genres.

HORROR IN AUSTRALASIA

Australian cinema has suffered from many of the problems that plague other English-language-speaking countries, primarily the domination of US product. Australian cinema slowly developed a voice of its own and much of its output is characterised by the harsh reality of colonial living, especially in the outback, so vast and so far from the civilisations of the mainly coastal cities. But it has also seen the loss of many of its successful actors and directors, lured by the bright lights of Holly-wood.

A key problem in discussing Australian cinema is finding a specifically Australian voice in a country whose films are often international co-productions. It wasn't until the 1970s that the Australian government gave its support to the development of an indigenous feature film industry. Although *Wake in Fright* (aka *Outback,* 1971) was directed by Canadian Ted Kotcheff and starred British actor Donald Pleasance, it nonetheless sparked the genesis of the Australian horror film. This nasty thriller about a violent outback town contains scenes of sinister customs and hostility towards outsiders.

Australia's best-known director Peter Weir also began working in the 1970s. *The Cars that Ate Paris* (1974), surely one of the greatest ever film titles, similarly features an isolated community, but one whose source of income derives from causing passing drivers to crash, then cannibalising their cars, enlarging the town with the crippled survivors of the 'accidents'. It's an atypically Australian tale of an isolated community at odds with city dwellers, but mixed with the auto-fetish ethos of JG

Ballard. Weir followed this with *Picnic at Hanging Rock* (1974), an evocative tale about a number of schoolgirls who mysteriously vanish whilst on an outing to Hanging Rock in 1900. The horror is far more cerebral than explicit, a wistful invocation of puberty in the desolate outdoors that lingers with the viewer like a half-remembered dream. Then came *The Last Wave* (1977) and *The Plumber* (1979), until Weir eventually moved away from Australia, and horror, to work in mainstream Hollywood.

Patrick (1978), directed by Richard Franklin, told the tale of a traumatised kid who develops psychokinetic powers as an adult. It's an unusual premise for a horror film as the perpetrator of the atrocities is immobile and comatose for the running time (a similar scenario was used in the British film *The Medusa Touch* [1978]). The film was produced by Anthony I Ginnane who went on to make a number of horror films amongst his prolific output, including the vampire film *Thirst* (1979), *Strange Behaviour* (1981) and *Demonstone* (1990).

Colin Eggleston's *Long Weekend* (1979) featured an irresponsible couple on a camping holiday slowly realising that the environment could bite back. Both tense and cleverly constructed, the couple's nemeses weren't obviously scary Australian creatures, but insects and birds instead. Eggleston went on to write and direct two similarly themed films: *Innocent Prey* (1984), in which a wife discovers that her hubbie is actually a serial killer, and *Cassandra* (1986), a slasher flick where a woman has to deal with a vicious murderer and dig up the ghosts of her past. Eggleston also directed the horror comedy *Outback Vampires* (1987), which, strangely enough, concerned a group of vampires based in the Australian outback, mixing graphic bloodletting with the laughs.

Brian Trenchard-Smith was another of the country's prominent directors whose gore-fest *Turkey Shoot* (1982) is a post-apocalyptic reworking of *Hounds of Zaroff* (1932), where humans, in this case a bunch of prisoners, become the hunters' prey. The film was amusingly re-titled *Blood Camp Thatcher* in the UK and was unamusingly censored (originally) of the only parts that make the film worth watching in the first place. Trenchard-Smith followed this up with the deranged *Dead End Drive-in* (1986) where drive-in cinemas are turned into concentration camps for the unemployed.

George Miller's *Mad Max* (1979) and its sequels, though not strictly horror films, had an enormous impact on the Australian film industry. These tense and exciting films pushed the boundaries of action and violence and used the outback to full effect for their themes of alienation. They proved that the Australian film could live up to its Hollywood cousin in terms of production values and box-office returns, values that would prove important to Russell Mulcahy's *Razorback* (1984), whose outlook was undeniably Australian.

The 1980s and 1990s were a boom time for Australian cinema where mainstream movies were at the height of public consciousness and many of its stars and directors were moving to Hollywood. Meanwhile, across a shorter stretch of water, avid movie buff and enthusiastic amateur filmmaker Peter Jackson had been turned down for a job at New Zealand's National Film Unit. He nevertheless continued making movies, spending four years working on the splatter comedy *Bad Taste* (1987). It was a labour of love, both for himself and his poor parents who often had to wait for their tea while his latex masks were baking in the oven. A near endless catalogue of depravity, *Bad Taste*'s baddies are evil aliens with builder's bum who drink vats of chunky vomit. Sheep explode, brains leak out of heads and guts are spilled liberally – causing the film to be banned or cut in many countries except, surprisingly, the UK. Jackson followed this up with *Meet the Feebles* (1989), a disgusting but highly amusing Muppet-esque story about a bunch of vile puppets, complete with a massacre and degenerate orgies. Then came *Braindead* (1992), his zombie splatterfest masterpiece.

A change of direction followed as Jackson turned to a quieter, disturbing horror with *Heavenly Creatures* (1994), starring Kate Winslet in an early role. It told the true story of two friends whose intense relationship leads to them murdering one of their mothers. It's a beautifully photographed work that perfectly blends the fantasy worlds of the two girls with their increasingly passionate obsession with each other. Although *The Frighteners* (1996), starring Michael J Fox, failed to ignite the box office, it bears all the hallmarks of Jackson's style, albeit slightly toned down in the gore department. The effects are astonishing, and pushed Weta Digital, the effects company Jackson created, to the limit. Weta are now the most successful CGI effects company outside the US, putting their talents to use in Jackson's *Lord of the Rings* (2001-2003) trilogy and his remake of *King Kong* (2005). Clearly a labour of love, Kong is rightly viewed by Jackson with a large amount of sympathy – after all, it's a bizarre love story as much as a monster movie – in between bouts of jaw-ripping, car-trashing, chest-thumping mayhem.

After the turn of the century some fresh Aussie blood hit the horror scene. Taking their cue from Peter Jackson, *Undead* (2003) was an ultra-cheap splatter comedy directed by twins Michael and Peter Spierig. James Wan and Leigh Whannell had met at film school in Melbourne and together crafted the short film *Saw* (2003). This led to them scripting the modestly budgeted, Hollywood-produced *Saw* (2004), which was the horror sleeper hit of its year – a bloody and claustrophobic game of torture and manipulation. In one scene someone needs to search through the entrails of a dead body in order to find the key that will free them, in another a man must saw off his own foot or die. The ringmaster for these sick games is 'Jigsaw', seen through ill-received television transmissions as a wooden dummy. The combination of nasty at exactly the time that audiences were turning away from implied horror mixed with a deliberately convoluted denouement that defied genre conventions made the film more than just a novelty.

Saw II (2005) and *Saw III* (2006) followed, the latter gaining press attention due to accusations that it was so vile that ambulances had to be called to some UK cinemas to assist audience members who had fainted at the sheer nastiness of it all. Such concerns only fuelled the box office further. The film's total lack of character development (which made the first films more engagingly unpleasant) removes any sense of sympathy leaving the audience free to enjoy the atrocities on show, including ripped-open chests and a man who comes close to being drowned in puréed pig carcasses. That's rancid puréed pig carcasses, just in case it wasn't revolting enough. Further cinematic brutality came in the shape of Greg Mclean's *Wolf Creek* (2005), a return to outback horror, which he followed up with *Rogue* (2007), a thriller about a man-eating crocodile.

The Last Wave (1977), Australia

Directed by: Peter Weir
Starring: Richard Chamberlain, Olivia Hamnett

The Last Wave contains elements of Weir's earlier films whilst maintaining an edge of almost nonchalant surrealism. David is a tax lawyer who takes on a murder/manslaughter case in which an aboriginal city dweller appears to have been drowned after a bar-room altercation. Dave suffers from nightmare visions that increasingly invade his waking world and he is convinced that they relate to his current case, despite the fact that he has had 'dreamstate' premonitions in his past. Weir creates a mundane world where the extraordinary is all too likely, filling his canvas with discreetly distanced shots to entice the viewer into the realism of his vision. This is a land where trust is all, where secrets must be kept under threat of death. Dave is appropriate for the job (he has the gift of foresight which is unheard of in a non-native) but is woefully unprepared (he is a tax lawyer and his social position isolates him from aboriginal society). The omens are writ large – violent hailstorms, black rain and inexplicable thunderstorms devoid of clouds show man's insignificance to the greater natural cycle. Dave's dreams hint of aboriginal figures breaking their vows and offering the secrets of the impending apocalypse in rain-drenched shadow.

In the film's most astonishingly prophetic scene Dave notices his car radio gushing water only to look up and see the people in the street floating, drowned, underneath the massive tidal wave that has engulfed the city, drifting past his windscreen wipers like abandoned helium balloons. The final scenes are underplayed to a degree that makes them almost arthouse but the combination of impending dread, ritualism, murder by psychosis and Armageddon make *The Last Wave* one of the more thought-provoking and devastating films of its era.

Razorback (1983), Australia

Directed by: Russell Mulcahy
Starring: Gregory Harrison, Arkie Whiteley, Bill Kerr, Chris Haywood, David Argue, Judy Morris

Beth Winters, an animal welfare reporter, goes to the outback town of Gumalla, 'an aboriginal word meaning "guts"', to investigate the kangaroo slaughter industry. At the unsanitary abattoir she has a run-in with Benny and Dicko, but their attempts to rape and murder her are curtailed by the appearance of a huge beast, who then savages her. Her husband is determined to get to the bottom of her disappearance and soon finds himself in the company of Jake, a boar-hunter on a personal quest to find the razorback pig that killed his grandson two years earlier.

Although *Razorback* has the *Jaws*-like premise of a large beast, whose existence is denied by the townspeople, killing loners and being hunted down by an embittered victim of a previous attack, the animosity of the locals gives another dimension to its horror. The 900-pound killing machine is ostensibly the monster, but the real villains are the sadistic Benny and Dicko, rural psychotics so feared by city folk for their animal-istic ticks and glee at suffering.

Mulcahy's feature debut is a visually stunning feast, with deep-orange sunsets, stylised backlit fog and extensive use of colour filters to create an alien, surreal landscape full of skeletal trees, rusted agricultural machinery and sun-bleached bones that threaten to come to life under the hallucinations of dehydration. The razorback's attacks are carefully constructed sequences of mere glimpses and sound, either tearing through Jake's house in a sly aside to *The Evil Dead*, pulling the terrified

Beth from her car as she clutches wildly out of the shattered back window or wrenching half a makeshift house away, so that its owner sits dumbfounded as his walls and his television set recede into the distance. A slick blend of horror staples combined with pop video aesthetics and a killer pig, what's not to like?

Braindead (1992), New Zealand

Directed by: Peter Jackson
Starring: Timothy Balme, Elizabeth Moody

Lionel's mummy isn't too well. In fact she's dead, infected by the bite of a Simian Raticus while spying on her son. She's currently sharing her cellar with an increasing population of zombies and it's down to Lionel to keep them fed, sedated and out of trouble.

One of the goriest, most disgusting, entrails-spilling, head-chopping splatterfests to get a commercial release, *Braindead* is irresponsibly and gratuitously violent. It's also wildly inventive, brilliantly designed and very, very funny. Jackson's debut film, the appropriately named *Bad Taste*, similarly features a phenomenally high gore rating but is essentially a comedy too. Never one to keep the camera still, and always choosing the most grotesque angles with which to fill the screen, Jackson's characters are all larger than life, from the pasty-faced mother with her diminishing number of appendages to the vigilante vicar who 'kicks arse for the lord' before becoming a very randy zombie, enjoying noisy sex with an almost decapitated nurse. She quickly conceives a zombie baby whose cannibalistic park-stroll outings result in mayhem. When Lionel's uncle's party gets into full swing, the violence reaches astronomical levels; half heads slide around the floor like pucks, whole ribcages are wrenched from bodies, heads split open, entrails strangle the living and the place is so awash with bodily fluids that Lionel can't run because the floor is so slippery. If this sounds revolting, it's because it is, but it is made with such impish glee you end up grinning wildly at every new atrocity. Fortunately the BBFC saw the joke and released the film uncut, but the MPAA had a serious humour bypass, reducing the film's running time by over 20 minutes.

Undead (2003), Australia

Directed by: Michael Spierig, Peter Spierig
Starring: Felicity Mason, Mungo McKay

A shower of meteorites instigates a deadly infection that causes sufferers to spread the disease by chowing down on living flesh. Having decided to leave the quiet fishing town of Berkley, René discovers that getting out can be harder than she imagined when the undead are on the loose and seemingly unstoppable. That's unstoppable to all bar the maverick three-barrelled-gun-toting nutcase who, along with the last remaining survivors, holes up in a farmhouse to find the cause of the outbreak.

Undead is a hoot from start to finish, an unabashed freewheeling gore flick that tips its wide-brimmed hat to everything from *Braindead*, *Return of the Living Dead* (1995), *Close Encounters of the Third Kind* (1977) and *Versus* (2000) but has enough sense to mix genres to novel effect. This is an alien abductee (even the crickets get beamed up) zombie film that's chock full of special effects – remarkable considering the sub-$1million budget. When René is stopped by a traffic accident her companion becomes infected, only to be blown clean in half by Marion's modified gun, his legs dancing around as his spine still protrudes upwards. Brains are punched through heads. There's meltings and exploding body parts galore, limbs wrenched from sockets and plenty of internal organs sloshing around the screen. But the whole thing is pulled off with *joie de vivre* and the surrounding conspiracy plot raises the film above mere pastiche. As with Jackson's *Bad Taste*, this was a film that took years to make – the effects work was rendered on a home computer – although the twins' budget and previous advertising experience helped greatly. Twenty-first century DIY filmmaking at its best.

Wolf Creek (2005), Australia

Directed by: Greg McLean
Starring: John Jarratt, Cassandra Magrath, Kestie Morassi, Nathan Phillips

The feature debut of Greg McLean, *Wolf Creek* is initially a slow-burning horror film that wrongfoots the viewer as much as it does the protagonists – although we don't have to suffer their pain and torture! The tale, 'based on true events', has all the elements of a simple campfire tale with the relevance of a contemporary setting. Once more the Australian outback is a metaphor for lawlessness and isolation as Ben buys a car to drive two English girls to the impressive crater at Wolf Creek. When they return from exploring the area they find that the car has packed in. As luck would have it a passing local, Mick, offers to tow the car to his garage. But is it luck? When the three wake up after a suspiciously deep sleep they find themselves trussed up near an abandoned mine and at the mercy of a sadistic killer with the trophies of previous unfortunates lying dismembered and decomposing in his workshop of despair.

In taking time to establish his characters on their road trip McLean makes sure that the audience identify with them as rounded and believable human beings. The villain of the piece is initially so amiable that when his true intentions are revealed the crimes become all the more ghastly. He is completely devoid of emotional understanding, treating human beings the same way he treats the kangaroos that plague the desert regions. Mick's motives are sexual in nature but mixed with sadistic power play. The matter-of-fact way he prevents one of the girls escaping by telling her the technique of severing spines whilst administering that very process is one of the film's most chilling moments. A sick, taut and visceral piece that shows the art of low-budget filmmaking is not dead.

References

1. Quotation from *Hellraiser* (1987)
2. Thomas Schatz, *Hollywood Genres*, Random House, 1981, p18
3. Quotation from *Frankenstein* (1931)
4. Quotation from *Carnival of Souls* (1962)
5. Alfred Hitchcock, *Hitchcock by Truffaut*, Paladin Books, 1984, p91
6. Quotation from *Scream* (1996)
7. David Cronenberg, Excerpt from interview in *Mondo 2000*
8. Quotation from *Halloween* (1978)
9. Based upon Coffin Joe article written by the authors which first appeared on www.kamera.co.uk and reproduced with permission
10. Stephen Teo, *Hong Kong Cinema, The Extra Dimensions*, BFI, 1997, p219
11. Government of India Central Board of Film Certification: http://www.cbfcindia.tn.nic.in/
12. Ibid

BIBLIOGRAPHY

Boot, Andy, *Fragments of Fear An Illustrated History of British Horror Films*, London, Creation Books, 1996

Eyles, Allen, Adkinson, Robert, Fry, Nicholas (Eds), *The House of Horror, The Complete Story of Hammer Films*, New York, Lorrimer, 1984

Hardy, Phil (Ed), *The Aurum Film Encyclopedia Horror*, London, Aurum, 1996

Herzogenrath, Bernd, *The Films of Tod Browning*, Black Dog Publishing, 2006

Jones, Stephen, *The Illustrated Vampire Movie Guide*, London, Titan Books, 1993

Le Blanc, Michelle and Odell, Colin, *Horror Films*, Harpenden, Pocket Essentials, 2000

Manvell, Roger (Ed), *The International Encyclopedia of Film*, London, Rainbird Reference Books, 1972

Mathews, Tom Dewe, *Censored. What They Didn't Allow You to See, And Why: The Story of Film Censorship in Britain*, London, Random House, 1994

Newman, Kim (Ed), *The BFI Companion to Horror*, London, BFI, 1996

Nowell-Smith, Geoffrey (Ed), *The Oxford History of World Cinema*, Oxford, Oxford University Press, 1996

O'Brien, Daniel, *Spooky Encounters: A Gwailo's Guide to Hong Kong Horror*, Manchester, Headpress, 2003

Odell, Colin and Le Blanc, Michelle, *Vampire Films*, Harpenden, Pocket Essentials, 2000

Schatz, Thomas, *Hollywood Genres*, New York, Random House, 1981

Schneider, Steven Jay, *Fear Without Frontiers*, England, FAB Press, 2003

Teo, Stephen, *Hong Kong Cinema, The Extra Dimensions*, London, BFI, 1997

Thrower, Stephen (Ed), *Eyeball Compendium*, Godalming, FAB Press, 2003

Tohill, Cathal and Tombs, Pete, *Immoral tales, Sex and Horror Cinema in Europe 1956-1984*, London, Primitive Press, 1994

Tombs, Pete, *Mondo Macabro, Weird and Wonderful Cinema Around the World*, London, Titan Books, 1997

Whitehead, Mark, *Slasher Movies*, Harpenden, Pocket Essentials, 2000

INDEX